Single Mother in Charge

Single Mother in Charge

How to Successfully Pursue Happiness

SANDY CHALKOUN

Women's Psychology

Michele A. Paludi, Series Editor

 **PRAEGER**

AN IMPRINT OF ABC-CLIO, LLC
Santa Barbara, California • Denver, Colorado • Oxford, England

Library of Congress Cataloging-in-Publication Data

Chalkoun, Sandy.
   Single mother in charge : how to successfully pursue happiness / Sandy Chalkoun.
      p. cm. — (Women's psychology)
   Includes bibliographical references and index.
   ISBN 978–0–313–38052–5 (hard copy : alk. paper) — ISBN 978–0–313–38053–2 (ebook)
1. Single mothers—Psychology. 2. Self-help techniques. 3. Self-esteem in women. 4. Happiness. I. Title.
HQ759.915.C475   2010
306.85′6—dc22   2010010701

ISBN: 978–0–313–38052–5
EISBN: 978–0–313–38053–2

14 13 12 11 10   1 2 3 4 5

This book is also available on the World Wide Web as an eBook.
Visit www.abc-clio.com for details.

Praeger
An Imprint of ABC-CLIO, LLC

ABC-CLIO, LLC
130 Cremona Drive, P.O. Box 1911
Santa Barbara, California 93116-1911

This book is printed on acid-free paper ∞

Manufactured in the United States of America

Contents

Acknowledgments

When I first began doing research for this book, about five years ago, my sole purpose was to figure out how the science of happiness can make me happier and increase my son's odds of being happy in his own life. But as the years passed, writing this book led to unintended lessons. I learned how to deal with my emotions and to trust my instincts. I learned how to be a better listener, a better student, and a better friend. I learned that there is always something *I* can do in any situation. I am grateful to have the opportunity to pass on these lessons to others through this book, but I have not done this alone.

Sarah, thank you for being the first to go through my initial messy pages. Debbie at Praeger, thank you for believing in this project from day one. Stephanie, you understood every word, thought, and emotion and gave me confidence to move forward. Though your name doesn't appear anywhere, you are "threaded" in every sentence. I am grateful for your wisdom and your friendship. Leo, Anna, and Linda, you helped me during difficult times and I will never forget that. Also, thanks to everyone at Kudoki. Aura and Nava, you have been dear friends, providing "therapy" to me whenever I needed it without judgment or criticism. Your support is priceless. To my parents, I thank you for being good examples of how to be optimistic and strong. These lessons have been very valuable to me. I know that it is difficult for children to realize all that has been done for them, so I thank you for what I know you've done, and for what I don't realize you've done for me. To my grandmother, Teta, may she rest in peace, thank you for teaching everyone around you the virtues of kindness and acceptance. Your silent wisdom has been a guide for me.

And to Mike, who has stood by my side these past few years with his unlimited capacity to offer words of wisdom, kindness, understanding, and motivation, you have my deepest gratitude and respect. I love your authenticity and how you seem to do everything so effortlessly and with so few words. I thank you for encouraging my freedom, helping me face my challenges, and allowing me to find my way in peace. As I always tell you, you are my favorite adult person in this world.

To Michael, my son, this book is for you. You inspired me to learn how to make the best of our lives. You gave me the strength to face all my challenges. My son, you have my unconditional and deepest love. You have a big heart, an amazing ability to learn and to communicate, and reasoning abilities beyond your years (not to mention your adorable smile). You are stronger than you know, and my belief in you is unshakeable. As your mother, I ask and encourage you to be true to yourself in your life, whatever you choose to do.

And to dear baby Eva, whom I never dreamed of having when I first started writing this book, I'm so happy to have you in our lives. I can't wait to keep spending time with your wise and joyful soul. I don't know how this book will serve you, but perhaps it can help you find your power in your own life. As your mother, I also ask and encourage you to be true to yourself in your life.

There are so many other family members, friends, and other people to thank in our lives that I do not have the space to mention. This includes people doing good research, a passerby who shows kindness, or other teacher giving life lessons. I try to show you gratitude in the moment, so your absence in this acknowledgments section has no meaning.

I also feel like I need to thank you, the reader, who may now choose to take some of my words and put them into practice to improve your life and that of your children. By doing so, this will affect not only you, but everyone around you as well as generations after you. This is a great gift to all human beings, and since I am one of them, I will take this opportunity to thank you in advance from the bottom of my heart.

Introduction: A Second Birthday

When my son was 11 months old his father decided, without warning or discussion, to leave our marriage. As we sat on the old wicker chairs on our balcony, he told me that I loved him more than he loved me. He told me that he no longer saw me as a woman, and that he wasn't happy. I was full of tears and despair, with a baby in my arms.

Now I celebrate that exact day, September 10, every year. I consider it to be my second birthday: the day I started learning how to live from scratch. I could never have anticipated how grateful I would eventually be that this "marriage" ended, even though it has meant living with the challenges of being a single mother. I remember being curled up in fetal position on the kitchen floor that week, sobbing my eyes out and trying to understand how all my dreams of a loving husband and close, happy family could vanish in a moment. In spite of how prevalent divorce is in our time, I could not help feeling ashamed that I had become a single mother, and I dreaded the pitying looks I expected to get whenever someone discovered this new information about me.

The pitying looks did come, and although I appreciated their empathy, I quickly came to resent the expectation from friends and strangers that my life must be miserable and that I should be unhappy. I became convinced that this did not have to be the case, and that I could hope for happiness as a single mother. I now know that I was right.

I began by realizing that my dream of an old-fashioned, married-for-life, close, loving, and happy family life was just a dream. It was not a true reflection of the sad reality of the marriage I had been living. It was time to let go of this "unreal" dream. I also realized that in order to have the strength to give my son a well-balanced and happy childhood, I would need to balance myself first. I would need to pick myself up and focus in a new direction.

It's so easy these days to focus on the negative aspects of life. People are always reminding you about some terrible thing they heard about. The news we are exposed to doesn't help. Reports tell us about the abusive teacher, not about the millions of honest and hardworking teachers inspiring students every day. The media inform us about the murder, not the millions of daily cooperative gestures between people. And they pound home the (incorrect) message that the life of a single mother is bound to be unhappy. Or, at least, substantially lacking.

My intention in this book is not to claim that being a single mother is paradise, or that it doesn't come with challenges. I'm not trying to claim that it's better to be a single mother than to be in a two-parent family or some other family unit. Nor do I claim to have a magic recipe for happiness. And my intent is certainly not to put pressure on you (or on myself) or on our children to achieve or arrive at anything. What I will do is share with you some ideas on how to *make the best* of the situation, whatever it is, and how not to simply accept old stereotypes about single motherhood.

I hope the book will answer certain questions for you such as: How can we come to fully accept our experiences? How can we and our children thrive in the face of so many challenges? Is it unrealistic to see the glass so full?

The stories of single mothers across this country may not be the same, but I suspect that we are not far apart in our experiences. Some of us may have left a marriage, or been left; others have been cheated on, or are widowed. Some of us have chosen to become single mothers. Some of us may have more income and some less. But our uniting factor is that we are women and mothers, likely playing the primary, if not the sole, role in parenting our children. What we also have in common is that we can improve our experience!

This book is designed to give you ideas, backed by scientific research, about how to improve your life. Most of these have worked for me, but you will need to explore which ones can work for you. It doesn't matter if you use some or all of these strategies; just start somewhere. The fact that you are reading this means that you are probably more ready than you know to take charge of your life.

I have no doubt that you will be able to draw from some of my experiences, and from those of the inspirational single mothers who have contributed to this book, many reasons to improve your attitude and your life. Of course, in doing so, you will inevitably improve the lives of your children.

But reading the pages of this book is *not* enough. If you really want to transform your life, you will need to incorporate the ideas into your routines. Theory is just theory. But put theory into practice and it could be life transforming! It's up to you . . .

SECTION 1

Three Fundamental Truths

Before exploring your past, or expecting to make any changes for your future, your mind has to be open to new ideas and new strategies. We are all able to learn and grow every day but we need to be open to new ideas to achieve this. What does it mean to be open-minded? I suppose it means looking at things with fresh eyes. Forget what you know, what you've seen, and even who you *are* for a moment. See yourself as an empty cup ready to be filled with new thoughts, ideas, and experiences.

It *is* possible for your life today to be different from yesterday and from the day before. In fact, every moment is an opportunity for newness and rebirth. You can decide to be whomever you want today. Fresh and new. The rest of your life starts now! Ready?

I'd like to start by offering up three fundamental truths that we all seem to know but also manage to ignore. Understanding these fundamental truths will open your mind to the possibilities offered in the rest of the book. Try to pause as you read. Take time between chapters to reflect, and even to sleep on it. The effects of what you learn can sometimes be slow and subtle, yet powerful and long-lasting. Transformation doesn't have to be through an "aha!" moment. It can be a gradual, step-by-step process, in which small changes are incorporated on a daily basis. You might even walk backwards sometimes (as I often do), and then leap forward. You might find there are days (or months) when you are simply pacing around in circles. But once you are on the right path, you will be amazed how determined you will be to stay on it!

FUNDAMENTAL TRUTH #1

What You Believe Will Control Your Life

Here's a list of the beliefs I held when I first became a single mother:

My son is going to be affected negatively by the divorce.

My son will grow up traumatized by what he saw.

My life is a mess.

I can't improve this situation.

Single mothers cannot create a stable home for their kids.

I'm unattractive.

It's awful to be a single mother.

My son will never have a normal sense of family.

I will never have a second child.

I can't exercise.

I can't do this by myself.

Can you relate? Perhaps you also have some of these common beliefs on your list? How about . . .

I can't succeed.

My kids will never have normal relationships as adults.

I can't make more money.

I messed everything up.

Before you can move forward, you'll need to challenge these beliefs. Why do you believe these things? Are they really true? And most importantly, how are these beliefs affecting your life? Your mind is a very powerful tool.

Consider this experiment performed on pregnant women in the United States in 1950 as an example of how the human body and mind can be shaped by belief. A group of pregnant women who were suffering from chronic nausea and vomiting were given a substance called syrup of ipecac and told it could cure their symptoms. What the women didn't know was that the syrup actually *causes* nausea and vomiting and is typically used to *induce* vomiting when toxic substances have been swallowed. The result? The effects of the medication was reversed and the nausea disappeared![1]

One of the subjects was a 28-year-old pregnant woman. Prior to taking ipecac, she didn't have gastric contractions (ipecac also interrupts normal gastric contractions, thereby inducing vomiting). Within 20 minutes of ingesting the drug, her nausea subsided and her normal gastric contractions resumed.[2] A drug that normally *causes* illness actually cured it because patients expected it to do so.

The beginning of your transformation begins with an honest analysis of your beliefs. They can affect everything you do without you realizing it. What do you believe about your life, your kids, yourself? What prejudices and misconceptions are you carrying around with you? Are you letting some of the common misconceptions bandied about by the media and others about single motherhood affect you? My guess is yes.

Consider the history of placebos, another way to trick the mind through the power of suggestion. The placebo, or sugar pill, is an inert substance given as a control to certain patients during a drug trial. They think they are getting the *real* drug, and, according to Herbert Benson MD, a Harvard Professor and the President of the Mind/Body institute in Boston, studies have shown over and over again that placebos can produce positive curative effects in the 40–90 percent range, even when treating serious conditions like angina pectoris, bronchial asthma, herpes simplex, and duodenal ulcers.[3] When individuals on placebo believe that they should be feeling something, they make their bodies respond to enable it to do so.

In my reading, I also came across many articles on the use of antidepressant drugs. Irving Kirsch, author of *Antidepressants: The Emperor's New Drugs? Exploding the Antidepressant Myth*, and his colleagues analyzed 38 published clinical trials involving more than 3,000 depressed patients. They found that 75 percent of the antidepressant effect was also produced by placebos—by simple sugar pills! They then used the Freedom of Information Act to get the data that drug companies had sent to the FDA to get approval of their medication. "What we found," Kirsch said, "was even more shocking that what our 1998 study had shown. The difference between drug and placebo was even smaller in the data sent to the FDA than it was in the published literature. More than half of the clinical trials sponsored by the pharmaceutical companies showed no significant difference at all between drug and placebo."[4] Nonetheless, the use of antidepressants has almost doubled in the United States between 1996 and 2005—from 5.84 percent to 10.12 percent (27 million people).[5]

It's actually amazing that research has even found that if a fake pill is more expensive, it can be more effective at reducing pain than a cheaper one![6] Duke University behavioral economist Dan Ariely, who supervised the study, says it well: "When you expect something to happen, your brain makes it happen."[7]

Interestingly enough, the nocebo effect is the opposite of the placebo effect, a kind of "power of positive thinking" in reverse. In nocebo studies, if a patient *disbelieves* in a treatment, his or her symptoms get worse. The patients are given a sugar pill, but because they have a negative attitude or belief about what they think they are taking, their symptoms get *worse*. "They're convinced that something is going to go wrong, and it's a self-fulfilling prophecy," said Arthur Barsky, a psychiatrist at Boston's Brigham and Women's Hospital and author of *Stop being Your Symptoms and Start being Yourself*.[8] An extreme example of the nocebo effect is dying from fear after being bitten by a nonvenomous snake,[9] or people getting sick or dying after being hexed because of their belief in voodoo, otherwise known as voodoo death.

I actually have a bit of personal experience with this. When a 35-year-old friend of mine was trying to get pregnant, she saw fertility experts who had convinced her that her chances of getting pregnant were about 1 percent. She and I were the same age, and I suspected this statistic was incorrect and probably a ploy by the fertility clinic to get her to consider their profit-making procedures. With just a few minutes of Google research, I showed her that this statistic was incorrect and I changed her belief. She was pregnant a month later. Perhaps it was chance, but the ample studies on the nocebo effect make me think the power of belief played a role.

Here's another amazing example: according to research from the Framingham Heart Study, women who *believe* they are prone to heart disease are nearly four times as likely to die as women who didn't think were prone to the disease—even if they have the same blood pressure and cholesterol levels for their weight and age.[10]

Similarly, Herbert Benson says that surgeons are "wary of patients who are convinced that they will die." And, he adds, if they want to die in surgery in order to recontact a loved one, they are almost 100 percent likely to.[11]

If negative thoughts can actually kill you, then surely there is limitless power to what you believe. Before you can move forward, you'll have to reexamine these ideas, and this book will challenge you to do just that. As you read the following stories and research, ask yourself what you believe is true. Ask yourself what you believe is impossible. And then open your mind to a life filled with possibilities!

Earlier, I shared with you some of my old beliefs about being a single mother. These are the beliefs that I *now* hold:

I can be happy in my current situation.

My son will be OK.

I'm doing a good job as a mother in this circumstance.

I am strong.

I believe in myself.

I have good instincts.

I can do this.

I deserve to have good things happen.

So what *do* you believe? Perhaps it's time to rethink your past in order to redesign your future. You are the only one who can question and alter your beliefs. Write them down and really assess each belief. Ask a friend if they can go through them with you so you can get an objective opinion. Then read the remainder of this book with a fresh mind. Open up! Let some new beliefs replace some of your old ones. If you can do just that, my mission will have been accomplished. It's up to you . . .

Fundamental Truth #1: What You Believe Will Control Your Life

FUNDAMENTAL TRUTH #2

Being Positive Will Improve and Extend Your Life

There are two ways to live your life. One is as though nothing is a miracle. The other is as though everything is a miracle.

—Albert Einstein[12]

A study of the sisters of Notre Dame in Milwaukee was able to divide the convent into "happy" and "not so happy" nuns. Researchers examined the nuns' diaries dating right back to when each nun joined the order in the 1930s, counting how many times each used positive and negative words in describing their lives in the cloister. The daily routine of the nuns was identical—they ate the same food, did the same tasks, and had very similar life experiences. Yet there was a marked difference in their life expectancy. Two-thirds of the "not so happy" nuns died before their 85th birthday, while 90 percent of the "happy" nuns survived that milestone. The research found that, on average, the happiest nuns lived about nine years longer than the least happy nuns.[13] Nine years is a remarkable difference considering that smoking 25 cigarettes a day for 10 years is said to take about 3 years off your life.[14]

Although there may be good reasons to sometimes focus on negative emotions—research is increasingly focusing on how a positive attitude can change the entire course of our lives for the better. This relatively recent field of study is known as *positive psychology*.

Whereas traditional psychology focuses on negative experiences such as depression, psychosis, schizophrenia, or phobias, positive psychology investigates the fundamental roots of kindness, success, strength, virtues, well-being, and so on. So, for example, where traditional

FIGHT THE FLU WITH A SMILE

Researchers have new evidence of the link between positive emotions and physical health. In one study, 52 volunteers were vaccinated against the flu at the same time. The researchers also measured the brain activity of the volunteers using brain-imaging techniques during different emotional tasks, such as remembering happy or sad events. The scientists wanted to see whether people who show greater activity in the left side of the prefrontal cortex of the brain (linked to positive emotional responses) would be more immune to the flu after vaccination. Six months later, those whose brain imaging indicated they were happier (greater activity on the left side) were also found to have more antibodies protecting them against the flu.

Source: Psychology Today staff, "Smile Away the Flu," *Psychology Today*, September 9, 2003, http://www.psychologytoday.com/articles/pto-20030909 -000001.html. Last accessed March 18, 2010; "Study shows brain activity influences immune function," University of Wisconsin-Madison news, September 2, 2003, http://www.news.wisc.edu/8849. Last accessed March 18, 2010.

psychologists might study why children *fail* in school, their positive-psychology counterparts might study why kids *succeed.*

The very idea of delving into positive, not negative, topics seems somewhat revolutionary to this scientific community itself. Psychologist David Myers of Hope College USA looked at how often certain phrases have appeared in well-known scientific magazines. It turns out that since 1887, *Psychological Abstracts* has mentioned the term "anger" in some 14,889 articles, "anxiety" 93,371 times, and "depression" 120,897 times. Only 1 out of every 17 articles referred to positive feelings and emotions such as "joy" (1,789 times), "life satisfaction" (6,255 times), and "happiness" (5,764 times)."[15]

Positive psychology tries to figure out the scientific basis for why humans flourish and thrive, what strengths and virtues enable people to achieve satisfaction in life. Not surprisingly, it's a concept that seems to be catching on. The course Positive Psychology at Harvard University, taught by Tal Ben Shahar Ph.D. author of *Happier* and *The Pursuit of Perfect*, is now the largest at the school.

According to the experts, there are many good reasons for being optimistic:

People with a high level of optimism are more resilient.

Positive people generally live happier lives.

People who are optimistic are less likely to be depressed.

People who are optimistic work harder and succeed more.

Happy people heal faster.

Happy people are more likely to be leaders at work.

Optimism has also been linked to "perseverance and effective problem solving; academic, athletic, military, occupational, and political success; popularity; good health, and even to long life and freedom from trauma."[16]

Is it possible to be optimistic even if we don't feel it right now? Or when we are in the middle of a tough situation? The answer is "Yes!" Research has also shown that you are not just born with your level of optimism and then doomed to your current attitude. You can actually change how optimistic you are. Even if things don't feel very rosy right now, you can make changes that can improve your quality of life.

It is a truism that people who have "everything" in terms of money or career are sometimes very unhappy. Others may have "nothing" and are very happy. The approach to life is the critical difference.

Adopting a positive approach in your daily life as a single mother will improve your situation and that of your children dramatically. It doesn't mean that you won't have low or sad days. What it does mean is that you have the power to *increase* your happiness. Whatever it is right now, at least it will be an improvement. The goal is really to make the *best* of the situation.

Being positive does not mean you should live an illusion. It doesn't mean putting on rose-colored glasses or walking around with a fake or unrealistic smile. Being positive means being realistic, authentic and optimistic. Either you can see rain as something that's bad and worth complaining about, or

"We've spent years saying that giving up smoking could be the single most important thing that we could do for the health of the nation.

"And yet there is mounting evidence that happiness might be at least as powerful a predictor, if not a more powerful predictor than some of the other lifestyle factors that we talk about in terms of cigarette smoking, diet, physical activity and those kind of things."

—Dr. Derek Cox,
Director of Public Health at
Dumfries and Galloway[17]

you can see rain as watering our plants and offering a good excuse for a cozy day at home. There is no right or wrong; it's just how you view life.

If this book achieves anything, I hope it might help you rebalance your own negative image of single motherhood by providing information, research and perspectives that are positive about the experience. By being exposed to the positive, rather than purely focusing on the negative, you can regain balance and hope. Since there are already plenty of negative stereotypes about being a single mother, there is no need for me to spell these out in detail. Therefore, you will get only the "good stuff" in these pages—I'll leave it to the rest of the world to try to fill our heads with negativity (which I usually tune out). At the end of this journey, you may even find, as I have, that your ordeal ultimately changed you for the better!

Fundamental Truth #2: Being Positive Will Improve and Extend Your Life

FUNDAMENTAL TRUTH #3

Actions Can Breathe Life into Your Ideas

People often confide in me about business ideas they are considering, because they know I have legal training. Friends also often tell me about interesting ideas they might have read in a book. We discuss everything from investments to parenting to business.

What these conversations frequently have in common is that they are mostly talk and no action. Think of how many people you know "plan to be their own boss" or "plan to open a restaurant one day." It's easy to have ideas about something, but it's another thing to actually do it! The difference is critical. It's the difference between being a dreamer and a doer!

I learned a critical lesson about this after attending prenatal classes during my pregnancy. Among other things, we were shown some cheesy, old-fashioned videos about childbirth and breastfeeding that in no way prepared me for the task. After giving birth, I felt I'd been given extremely inadequate information about how to take care of a baby. I was mystified as to how I could have gone to all those classes and ended up knowing so little. I also quickly realized that new mothers have no time to read books when they have a baby. So I came up with the brilliant idea of creating a DVD on how to take a care of a newborn baby. I did a quick market research and found that there were *none* on the market. But I kept my idea to myself for several years and did nothing.

Years later, I read about two moms in my city, Montreal, who had produced a DVD on being a new mother. The DVD was doing really well and they had even managed to get it into Wal-Mart, Amazon.com, and other major retailers. On that day, I was not frustrated about my "secret" idea being done by someone else. I had learned a valuable lesson!

The lesson is that ideas, whether you invent them or get them from reading this book, are probably useless unless they are followed by action. This whole book will be useless in your life unless you apply the strategies in it.

Since that experience, I adopted a new habit that has served me well in work as well as personally. As soon as there's something I plan to do or I think is a good idea, I immediately **take action**. No matter how small that action is, I just get the ball rolling.

> "The most effective way to do it, is to *do* it."
>
> —Amelia Earhart[18]

This action can be small or large but it is *action*. I might register a Web site domain name, or write something in my agenda to do, even if it's a tiny step; for example, "research this topic," or "order this book," or "ask so and so about their experience in a topic."

You'd be absolutely amazed at the difference this makes! Taking an initial action, no matter how small, actually converts ideas into reality and brings them to life. They are no longer simply in your head. They have started coming to life. I invite you, while reading this book, to put it down and to go **do something** that comes to your mind. Make it real! Make it possible!

If you think you should reevaluate your beliefs after reading the earlier chapter on beliefs, then go to your agenda, choose a lunch hour, and write: "Buy a journal today and write down all my beliefs and question them one by one."

If you think or decide that you are watching too much TV or if you think you should sleep more, then put down your book, go to your bedroom, and remove the TV from that room. Right away! The mere fact of unplugging a TV reinforces your decision or idea with a concrete real act. Action!

Ask yourself what ideas you've had this past year. Did you do anything about them or did they simply stay lingering in your head? Do something today about one of them! The easiest first step would be to at least write them down and post them where you can see them in your bedroom.

In order to get into the habit of taking action, I also recommend that from this moment on, you get in the habit of doing what you say you're going to do. If you say you'll do something, then you should do it. If you don't plan on doing something, then don't say it. Keep your word. Once you get good at the habit of doing what you say, then your words become very powerful.

By the way, the DVD moms later branched out with a radio show about parenting and are now on their second successful DVD, and I am very happy for their success. They actually did it and deserve to reap the fruits of their labor. Bravo!

Fundamental Truth # 3: Actions Can Breathe Life into Your Ideas

SECTION 2

Empty Your Cup

In this Section, we will work on ridding ourselves of the most difficult residues from our negative experiences. Fear, anxiety, guilt, worry, and similar negative emotions are taking up space in our lives and are standing in the way. We need to empty our cup of these and balance ourselves to properly take care of our children. It's a simple equation: Happy mother = happy child. Miserable mother = miserable child.

As the renowned writer Krishnamurti says, "Without freedom from the past, there is no freedom at all, because the mind is never new, fresh, innocent."[1]

There is little room for anything else. Only when we have emptied these negative emotions from our cup can we attempt to fill it up with some positive strategies for being happier.

As the Dalai Lama teaches,

The first step in seeking happiness is learning. We first have to learn how negative emotions and behaviors are harmful to us and how positive emotions are helpful. We must also realize that these negative emotions are not only very bad and harmful to one personally, but are also harmful to society and the future of the whole world.[2]

CHAPTER 1

"I'm Afraid"

The first few years after separation from my son's father were incredibly difficult. Every interaction was charged with stress and emotion. Each pickup, drop-off, conversation, and change of schedule took over my life. Conflict, and the potential for conflict, sucked all my energy. It seemed as though I was living with a perpetual fight-or-flight response, and the lack of peace was overwhelming.

It came to a head one weekend when dealing with the typically supercharged issue of pickup and drop-off. We had disagreed about when I was supposed to pick up my son. He ordered me to come at a time of his choosing at the end of the weekend. I struggled with anxiety the whole weekend, wondering what to do. Should I go when he ordered me to? Should I go at the time that was, in my view, the correct time according to our legal agreement? Should I bring the police, to avoid possibilities of aggressiveness? Should I ask my dad to come with me? As usual, I was trying to solve a host of problems while avoiding conflict.

My stomach hurt, my thoughts were running at 100 miles a minute, and my heartbeat was rapid. Traumatizing memories from my marriage played themselves over and over in my head that weekend while I tried to work out different scenarios for the pickup. I was sweating and tense inside. And my stomach was churning and churning all weekend.

I had so many fears caught in that stomach blender. They had been there for years...

I was afraid of getting anyone mad.

I was afraid of what people would think.

I was afraid of what my parents would think.

I was very afraid of what my son would think.

I was afraid of how my actions might affect my son.

I was afraid of upsetting my son.

I was afraid of being an unfair person, even to my ex.

I was afraid of making mistakes or bad decisions.

And mostly, I was afraid of the unknown.

All these fears left me anxious, paralyzed, and unable to cope.

Nonetheless, on that fateful weekend, I made a decision. I went to pick up my son that Sunday night at the hour that *I* believed was the appropriate one. I decided to go *by myself*, with no one else, come what may! Believe me, it took all the courage I could muster to do it, given all that I was fighting inside.

Lo and behold, when I arrived to pick up my son, nothing happened. We did not speak a word. He simply handed my son over to me. Perhaps my unwillingness to be bullied was in my eyes. I'm not sure. But that night, the very uneventfulness was the *first step* on a long road of transformation from fearful to fearless, from worried to calm, from helpless to empowered. "Do the thing you fear most and the death of fear is certain," said Mark Twain.[3]

Taking that first leap ushered in me a desire to improve my life in all ways. I was on a new path. And though it has taken many years, and though I keep stumbling along the way, I have not left it since.

Years later, my curiosity about this weekend did not leave me. I still wondered what drove me to go alone despite all my fears? How and why was I able to make that decision? I did not just "deal with it," "get over it," "forget about it," or "fight my fears." This is *not* what happened. I desperately wanted to figure out how I did it so I could learn to deal with other "stomach blender" adversities and anxieties that kept coming up in my life, whether related to divorce or not.

After many years of contemplation and experiences with these and other similar issues, I found a very natural theory and solution to deal with them. Though many other theories exist on fear and anxiety, my approach has worked for me and the people with whom I have come into contact. There is no fighting or resistance involved in it. I offer it to you to try to deal with your own fears and anxieties.

I will describe the most essential part of this process in the next chapter, which is on *anxiety*. But before we get there, let us first understand *fear* a little bit better.

Let us begin with the most *primal fear*—the fear we feel when we are in danger. This kind of fear is *our friend*. It is a survival signal that might be signaling danger. It should not be belittled, diminished, or ignored but rather seen as a gift. This fear arises when something is wrong. It's an intuition, and it can help protect you from becoming a victim. Our muscles get tense, our heart rate increases, and our senses get sharp. These bodily changes (sometimes called fight-or-flight stress response) are believed to be necessary for our survival. When something is "not quite right," our intuition knows it even before we can pinpoint why that is. We know there is danger. This is something that will happen instinctively and should be respected, not questioned.

Gavin de Becker, a danger expert and author of *The Gift of Fear* (which I highly recommend to all women), writes extensively about this primal fear and the intuition that goes with it. He thinks we are all equipped with a weapon proven to prevent crime, and even picking dangerous partners, *before* it happens. We all have it. It's called the "gift of fear."

He describes the story of a woman named Kelly. A man offers to help carry her groceries into her apartment; she instinctively doesn't like the sound of his voice—her intuition is warning her. She tells him she doesn't need help and feels apprehensive—her intuition is warning her. He insists on helping, and she goes *against* her gut and lets him. By doing so, she let the rapist into her apartment.[4]

De Becker describes how we get signals prior to violence. Our intuition, he says, often tells us through apprehension or an eerie feeling about these previolence indicators. He points out that we should pay attention to our intuition, calling it "knowing without knowing why."[5] So instead of trying to analyze or explain the feeling, or ridiculing it, we should realize it is a powerful internal resource, a warning signal, and respect it.

Let us not ignore or dismantle our internal safety system by ignoring our intuition! It is there to help us deal with impending violence, it helps us choose the right people to be in our lives, and it sends alarms to us for all kinds of potential harm.

Just recently, as I turned the corner to go my car which was parked on a dark street, I felt something strange about the man standing there, though I did not know what it was. I told the person I was walking with, "That guy is up to something." But instead of *questioning* my instinct, or trying to rationalize that everything is OK, I *respected* my instinct; I decided to immediately turn around to walk the other way in order to face and confuse the potential attacker (and remove any surprise element he might benefit from). Lo and behold, the man, who was now right behind me and my friend, got confused, turned around himself, and walked the other way. There is no doubt in my mind we were about to be mugged or attacked, but I believe that respecting my intuition prevented this.

Our survival signals are innate. When we are dealing with *primal fear* and danger intuition, respecting our instincts is the best way to go. You don't even need to do anything consciously to become more alert. When something is wrong, seems "off" or "eerie," your warning system will *automatically* warn you. Every situation is different, but what you always have on your side is your primal instinct to deal with it. It might not be smart, for example, for you to meet your ex alone if your instinct tells you there is danger looming. Respect your instincts. Don't overanalyze them. It might just save you from danger.

So as far as danger of physical harm goes and the primal fear associated with that, I reiterate that I think **fear is our friend**. Respect those instincts.

Now, back to the *other* fears. I gave you a list of the ones I was dealing with in my head on that anxious weekend: fear of what people think, fear of getting anyone mad, fear of the effects on my son, etc. What are yours? The first step to dealing with those kinds of fears is to *identify* them clearly. This is no easy task. It took me a long time to come up with my list. Yours may not be the same. You will need to sit and feel them. Not sit and *think*, just sit and *feel*. Be natural. Ask yourself what you are afraid of and do not fight or force these answers. Try to forget what's right or wrong or what you *should* or *should not* be afraid of. Forget if it's rational or not. Simply identify what is actually there. Are you afraid of your children hating you? Losing your job? Dying alone? Etc. . . .

Take a piece of paper and write down everything you can think of. Be natural, authentic, and honest. Try to see these fears *as your friend* for now. These fears are giving you information. They are telling you what you feel. Write this list knowing that no one else will see it but you. No one will judge you. And do not judge yourself while doing it. Simply see it as a fact-finding exercise. Just state the truth of what fears you have at this moment. Nothing wrong about them, nothing right about them. Simply state what *is*. Listen to

> "The presence of fear means only that fear is present, and nothing more."
>
> —Zen Buddhist teacher Suzanne Segal[6]

yourself. When you do this in this fashion, you will see that the answers often come quickly.

When you've emptied your heart and come up with your list, the next step is very important. Take a deep breath . . . And now *accept* that you have these fears. Acceptance does not mean that you will live with them forever or not overcome them it. Acceptance means to accept they are currently there. It means not to judge them or fight this truth, but to accept it. Simply accept that they exist for the moment, as if you are a private investigator who found out some *facts*. It's simply the acceptance that something exists, without judging it in any way.

Now relax and put these "facts" on hold for a moment while we discuss the key topic *anxiety* in the next chapter.

CHAPTER 2

"I'm So Anxious"

In the years of turmoil after my separation from my son's father, I experienced anxiety attacks, and many moments when I felt that I was not fully functional. My stomach would constantly churn, and the lump in my throat would get bigger. I didn't always know what the exact source was or what to do about it. I knew that some of my anxiety might have come from the intimidation tactics being used on me. I also knew that I had the list of fears I told you about earlier. But what I *didn't* know was how to deal with this situation.

Anxiety is defined by many people in many ways, but I will describe to you how I have been able to deal with it when it creeps into my life. Anxiety is the knot in your stomach, the lump in your throat, the dread, anguish, the internal agitation, jitteriness, nervousness, uneasiness, apprehension, or defensiveness about something. It's not just the momentary stress of getting somewhere on time in the morning. It is a stomach churn that is *persistent*, keeps coming back, and *won't go away*. You are unsettled. Anxiety is draining. It could be about any issue in your life. Let's call it *"internal turmoil."*

What I have learned after many years is that it is not the *fears* that cause most of us a huge problem, but the *internal turmoil* about something. If you are afraid of spiders, this is a fear but it not necessarily a problem. I know someone who is very afraid of spiders but it's not a big deal. If she comes over and happens to see a spider, she is afraid for two minutes, we get rid of the spider, and life goes on as before. She has no *internal turmoil* about spiders. It is not having any significant impact on her life. She does not have the lumps in her throat and stomach churning of *internal turmoil*.

Fear can be seen as just one of the factors contributing to the *internal turmoil* we are feeling, but it is not the whole story, nor is it necessarily the most important part of the story. Making our list of fears is not enough, nor is it necessarily going to help rid us of the *internal turmoil*. We will have to look deeper, to see what is really going on. We need to figure out what is *really* causing the stomach to churn . . .

Try this with me. Is there something that has been causing you nagging and persistent internal turmoil? I will show you how I have learned to deal with mine.

I already spoke to you about that weekend that made me hyperanxious with my son's father, and how my mind was racing and my insides were churning. I also told you about the fears I was carrying around, and that I decided to go by myself to pick up my son. But what you *don't* know is the key element that made me rid myself from the anxiety that weekend. You don't know this key element in the story. You don't know *why* I was so anxious all weekend, and neither did I at that time. I thought I was so anxious because of the fears I listed earlier. Those should be enough, but they were not the reason! Looking back, I know that my anxiety was *not caused by the fears* I described to you. The anxiety was deeper than that. And how did I get to have the courage to go get my son by myself despite my fears? It is only in analyzing the *internal turmoil* that we can we truly understand this (and resolve it).

As I take you through the steps of that particular situation, try and see if you can follow these steps to discover the causes of any *internal turmoil* that is in your life.

STEP 1: SEE INTERNAL TURMOIL
AS YOUR FRIEND

If your insides keep nagging you, it is a message to you. It is signaling that something is wrong. Something is "off." *Internal turmoil* is your body and mind sending you information. It is a signal that something needs to be addressed differently. It is your friend! Do not fight it; welcome it! Like fear, we can see anxiety as a gift!

Once you welcome the turmoil instead of trying to avoid it, suppress it, ignore it, or control it, you can sit down and try to figure out why it is there. Get to the bottom of it! To do this, you will need to listen to yourself, *without judgment*, without any box, without care about what is right or wrong or how anyone might judge what you feel. Eliminate the word "should" from your vocabulary about emotions. One cannot say "I shouldn't feel ABC." The reality is that you *do* feel ABC so it's better to accept this reality and try to see why.

In fact, I would go even deeper and say that the key is not to look for what you *feel*, but rather, to look for what you *know*. You must simply listen and look for the truth. You must observe yourself without having any preconceived notions, conclusions, or prejudices. It's simple observation. It's funny, because when you look for it in this way, it tends to pop up very quickly, and there is a real quietness about it. You will feel very calm when you find it. The truth speaks in a whispering and calm voice.

It is your *intuition* that will be speaking to you. There is a false impression that people have that intuition, or your "inner voice," is irrational or emotional. In fact, your intuition is very rational and very perceptive. Your mind already knows all the data about a situation. It has millions of data points, and it has processed everything like a computer. It knows what happened, when and what everyone did, who said what, who felt what, who did what, and all the personalities involved in an issue. It knows everything about a situation.

Your intuition knows the right answer—the same way your intuition knows when someone looks untrustworthy as when we spoke about danger. Trying to rationalize or justify why your intuition says something is unnecessary! If you feel like a situation or person is unhealthy for your family, there might be a thousand subtle reasons your intuition knows this. You might not be able to pinpoint exactly why or formulate it into a sentence. And why should you? You body and mind has already found the answer! You just need to be aware enough of your inner voice in order to accept it.

So the next step is to find the source of the turmoil. *Internal turmoil* is often caused by one of these three possibilities, all of which have to do with knowing and respecting who you are.

YOU ARE NOT DOING WHAT YOU *KNOW* YOU SHOULD DO

On my weekend of extreme turmoil, the real reason my stomach was churning was not due to the fears, but rather because something was "off" inside me. My body was sending me the message, "You are going in the wrong direction;" "You are doing something very wrong and you **know it**!" And it was right! I realized that weekend that the way my life was going was self-destructive. I came to terms with the fact that my son really, I mean *really* needed me, and if I continued on my current path, I **knew** I would surely become so physically ill I would no longer be able to care for him. I **knew** that my health would take a downturn for the worse if I continued to be afraid of everything with constant nervous lumps in my throat. I **knew** I needed to be fully functional and earn enough money to support my son, since I had always had, and would probably continue to have, most of the financial and caregiving responsibilities. I also **knew** my son and I deserved happiness and a peaceful life and that what I was doing would not get us there.

My anxiety was caused because I was not doing what I **knew** I should do given the current situation. I was constantly engaging in issues with my son's father, I was questioning myself all the time, I was focusing on the wrong things, and I was not taking care of myself or my son's well-being properly. This was the true cause of my *internal turmoil*. Thank you "anxiety" for giving me the signals to make me realize all these things—allowing me to change my course!

A friend had a similar stomach churning incident that was a result of not doing what she **knew** she should do when she was driving back early from a vacation with her kids in order to close a sale in her real estate job. Her anxiety level had reached an all-time high. She **knew** her job was causing her to neglect her challenged son and, since her family could afford it, she **knew** she should quit the job. She **knew** it was not worth it. Her anxiety was caused by not doing what she **knew** she should do. Thanks "anxiety" for pointing this out and showing her what the better path for her family is.

You Are Going Against Your Own Values

Our stomachs also become a blender and cause internal turmoil when we go against our *own* values, whatever they might be. When there is a conflict against our value system, this causes our insides to fight us back. There is no amount of meditation, relaxation, or exercise that can eliminate this *internal turmoil* until you resolve the conflict with your own values. A value isn't what is right or wrong in society, but what's right and wrong for *you*. No matter how strong you think you are, there is one battle you will never win, the battle against your own values.

Back to that weekend, in my case, the fact that I had become *so afraid* was against my own values. I am a person who is not fearful by nature, and I was going against my internal sense of self by allowing myself to be so afraid of my son's father, afraid of what people think, or anything else. I was being a victim, and this was not true to my nature. This is what was causing my *internal turmoil*. Once I realized this, I knew that I wanted to go *by myself* to pick up my son. This was my true nature. I didn't want to be afraid or to be a victim. It is not who I am.

Lisa (not her real name) is in a difficult marriage and was suffering anxiety about how the conflicts were escalating in her home. Her anxiety was leaving her with heart palpitations, and she was starting to become dysfunctional. What she discovered however, after making a list of her fears, is that her fears were not the underlying cause of her anxiety. What caused her anxiety was that she was doing things against her own values, against her own grain. She was reacting to her husband in ways that were not true to her nature, with anger and vengeance, and she was constantly being a hypocrite, against her own authenticity. It was not the fears of conflict escalation or potential divorce that were killing her inside. It was going against her true nature. Once she realized this, she resolved to find ways to cope that would not go against her nature. And she felt much better. Thank you anxiety for helping her look for better ways.

You Are Denying Something that You "Know"

Internal turmoil also comes up, as your *friend*, to tell you that you are not acknowledging something that you know is true. This is a very difficult one to understand. But accepting our fears allows us to look deeper. They can sometimes give us a clue to something we are "denying"—some difficult truth sitting there yearning to come out.

A clear example is Rina (not her real name), who is suffering from an illness. She was afraid of many things: her future, finances, her children's well-being, etc. You would think these fears would be the cause of the anxiety she was feeling. But in fact, when doing the self-awareness, she discovered that her stomach churning was coming from denying a difficult truth—that she might be *causing* part of her symptoms as a convenient excuse not to live. She realized this was connected to self-worth issues connected to her childhood. This is a very difficult truth to see. It takes great courage to admit to things to yourself that are difficult to see.

In my case, I had to stop denying a truth—that I was living another illusion. As I mentioned earlier, I used to carry around the dream of having a "nice, normal family with two or three children and a loving husband." This dream was hard to give up when I got separated. But then I switched to dreaming of having a "nice and cooperative divorce" for the sake of my son. I knew that this was better for him than parents who have noncooperation. I wanted so much to achieve this kind of harmony for the sake of my son often accepting and regularly putting up with intimidation and unfriendliness as a result. I had to face the truth that my expectation that we be "friendly" was completely unrealistic, another illusion. In my case, I had to face the difficult truth that I was denying.

Difficult things to admit can be anything: someone in your surroundings is mentally ill or disturbed, accepting traits of family members, acknowledging that you are participating in your own misery, accepting that certain relationships are not healthy, accepting that you have been affected by things in your childhood, etc.

Realizing that you have not been doing what you *know* you should do, or that you are going against *your* values, or that you have denied something you *know*, are really all part of the same strategy: Accepting yourself. Stop allowing others to judge you. Stop judging yourself. Understand yourself instead. Accepting the truth of who you are—accepting a truth that you have kept away from your heart. *This is what will stop the anxiety*. It is not a coincidence that 12-step programs always end their sessions with acceptance prayers.

Once you have done this exercise and realize and accept where the anxiety is from—once you have found the truth—you will be relieved. Even though your problem might not be solved, you are no longer dealing with a ghost but some reality. Once we have *reality* in front of us, and all the facts are clear, most of us know what actions we will want to take.

Once Rina realized she might be causing her own illness, although it was a difficult truth to admit, she was glad to have faced this truth. It relieved her anxiety and gave her courage to evaluate and do something about the situation.

Once I knew that my nature is not to be afraid and that I needed to get better to make sure I can take care of my son, all my fears seemed less important. I was less concerned about what anyone thought or who got mad. I was less worried about making mistakes. The answers started coming naturally to me.

You can see how fears are not truly the obstacle. They are just part of the facts of the story. Once you have found the truth of what caused your internal turmoil, you will *know* what to do. And this is

> It takes courage to grow up and become who you really are.
>
> — e. e. cummings[7]

where it will take courage. It takes courage to do what you *know* you should do. It takes great courage to be true to yourself. Courage is not to conquer fear—it is knowing and staying true to ourselves and charging forth anyway!

After figuring out all of the above, I knew what I needed to do, and found the courage to do it, in the presence of my fears.

I knew I needed to go to pick up my son alone that weekend to be true to myself—and I did.

I knew I needed to learn how not to engage in conflict or be intimidated anymore—and I slowly did. I refused to engage in many situations, minimized contact, dealing with issues only by e-mail, and refused to have conversations in my son's presence. Slowly, surely, over many years, I began to reclaim my space. I took charge of my home space, my phone, and my peace.

I knew I had to ensure my son's well-being and I started to. I started basing all my decisions on a simple formula—what is in my son's interest? Others opinions of me, whether or not my actions angered anyone, and a host of other considerations, became less relevant.

I also knew I needed to get better to ensure my son's well-being—so I started learning about positive psychology and ended up writing this book, which I hope will help others do the same.

I am not special—if I was able to make these changes, so can you! The next time you feel anxious, have a fight-or-flight type of feeling, tense headaches, or anxiety, don't fight it. Although there may not be *physical* dangers present, this is a message that there is a threat to your emotional and mental well-being. See these symptoms *as your friend* trying to guide you to make better decisions in your life by acknowledging the truth, living true to your values, and being true to yourself.

Take charge of your emotional life for the sake of your children. You are equipped with the internal signals to guide you. Trust them, have courage and faith in yourself, and the knots in your stomach will untie.

Put your future in good hands—your own.

—Author unknown

CHAPTER 3

"I'm So Angry"

Anger is a double-edged sword. It can be your red flag that something is wrong and motivate you to do something about it, like anxiety. But, like other negative emotions, it can also be detrimental to your health and relationships.

There is endless research showing the connection between poor health and anger, thus the importance of finding a way to deal with it. A study done at Ohio State University and published by the British journal *Brain Behaviour and Immunity* was one of the first controlled experiments linking anger and the physical healing of wounds. The researchers enlisted 98 volunteers, who agreed to receive minor burns on their forearms. Their skin was then monitored to see how quickly it healed. Each volunteer had been tested psychologically beforehand to measure how easily and often they got angry and if they had control over their anger. The results indicate that those who were ranked low in anger control were *4.2 times* likelier to need more than four days for their wounds to heal.[8] Of course, this study deals with external cuts and wounds. You can just imagine the effect of anger on your internal constitution!

If we truly want to rid ourselves from anger, even the bottled up kind, this is what has worked for me:

The first step is to identify what you *think* you are angry about. Is it that:

- he left you?
- he cheated on you?

- he leaves all the responsibility of the kids to you?
- you took care of him for years and he did nothing for you?
- he abused you?
- you have no time for yourself or to take care of yourself?
- he neglects his children?
- he bad-mouths you to your children?
- he's irresponsible?
- your parents aren't helping you enough?
- your friends don't understand?
- all of the above?

I suspect that at least some of these are common for many single mothers. (It simply amazes me how many single mothers seem to have similar stories.)

Many people will say that you have every "right" to be angry at these things, and that it's normal given what "he" or "they" have done, but I will challenge you to go further and deeper. The list I mentioned above is just a list of the "facts" or "events" which can lead to anger. Though they might look like the cause, they often are not. The real cause is often deeper. And when we look deeper, we can find an underlying feeling that is closer to the heart. We need to figure out what *we are feeling*, not what "they did."

To do this, we will need to do the same exercise as we did under *anxiety*. In other words, we need to figure out the underlying cause, feeling or source. To do this, you will need to sit in the anger, accept it, not judge it—not try to "control" it or "manage" it. In order not to judge it, you must eliminate thinking in "should" language—saying things like "I should" or "I shouldn't" be angry.

Being non-judgmental of the feeling is key to finding the source. Sources or feelings underlying anger might be feelings of "helplessness," "unfairness," "hurt," "humiliation," or, very often, an earlier childhood or other pain. By opening up your heart to allow the truth to come in without trying to control it, you are more likely to find it. And once you find the underlying feeling, you will be able to look for different solutions to alleviate that pain.

Let's see some examples:

Amanda (not her real name) is dating a new guy that she really likes. He was invited to a work-party and he did not invite her to come along.

Rather, he came to her house after the party with flowers and told her about how he told his friends at the party all about her. When he told her this, she was so upset that he didn't invite her. When she delved deeper and deeper, she started figuring out why. She realized that for her, his actions meant that he was trying to separate work from personal life or family. This realization is already quite closer to the truth, and further from the initial "angry" reaction. But in fact, her feelings were even *deeper*. When reflecting about what it would mean to her if work and family are separated, she realized that this meant he only wants a part-time family, which she did not want. If you delve even *deeper* into her childhood, she would tell you that she had a "part-time" family with her parents constantly leaving without warning for work for months at a time and leaving her with her grandmother. So what was no more than not being invited to a party from a new boyfriend, and although he showed so many signs of lovingness, this triggered anger her because she perceived a threat, the threat she felt as a child being in a part-time family. She became tense, unfriendly and didn't even realize why at the time. When reflecting, it became clear. She understood that past feelings come up in the present but that we can identify them if we are open to do so. This is what therapy achieves for many people. But with the right self non-judgmental approach and openness, you can achieve the same by yourself.

Once she realized this, she was able to become aware that the current situation is not the past and therefore be in the present.

Here is another example. Pamela (not her real name) got very upset at her son one day and intuitively knew that her anger was "off." She decided to allow herself to experience the feeling and to reflect on what she felt underneath the anger. This is *facing* an emotion. When reflecting non-judgmentally on herself, she realized that she was very sensitive to people not being considerate of her feelings because she didn't feel understood as a child and her feelings were not considered in her marriage. So when her son showed lack of consideration, this triggered very strong feelings. When she realized this, she was able to understand that she is reacting to the past and became aware of this trigger for the future. She was able to see that this current situation with her son was not the past situation and that children disregard feelings of others sometimes. Her reaction would have been more "tempered" had she been aware of her internal feelings and connections with the past.

When she apologized to her son, this was a deep apology. It was not what I consider to be a "false" apology of doing harm then apologizing, then doing harm, then apologizing and continuing this pattern (common in domestic abuse situations). A deep apology is one which was preceded by true reflection, understanding of the cause and effect of one's actions, and with a commitment to continually be aware of the triggers and prevent reoccurrence.

Through awareness of our internal feelings we are able to prevent future occurrences. Though doing these exercises can sometimes be painful, since they entail having to review and relive past pain, doing so stops the cycle of living in the past, unconsciously. With awareness of the cause, we can understand what triggers us and find methods to prevent reoccurrences, and avoid getting unnecessarily angry the next time.

Does this mean that the girlfriend or the mother described above should feel nothing about the boyfriend not inviting her to the party, or the child being inconsiderate? No. It means they can respond to it if they feel something, but the response will be appropriate to the situation and reflect the *current* reality of what happened and not get mixed up with other past issues. They would still express whatever concerns they had but the reaction would not have been as intense or panicked.

Intense emotions are a call to reflect on the self. If you are able to reflect and get to the source of issues by yourself or with the help of a non-judgmental empathetic friend (wonderful gift of life if you have one), then this is the finest of internal medicine. Your anger will dissipate with such deep understanding of the self. If not, you might need a therapist to help.

After the birth of her child, single mother by choice Kelly (not her real name) from Toronto found herself depressed and angry at the lack of support from her immediate family. She was able to identify the source of her anger and find comfort and solace through joining a support group for recently divorced and separated women. "Emotionally, the feeling of needing a place where your feelings could be validated and acknowledged was so important. And I think there was a lot of anger about feeling so isolated. Anger at all those that I thought and expected would be supportive ... " Eventually she came to the realization that she could get an even clearer idea of what was driving her anger through one-on-one therapy.

If you don't find the source of anger by yourself, through a friend or therapy, you might end up stuck in the analysis and unable to get to the bottom of things and this is very unhealthy! University of California–Riverside professor of psychology Sonja Lyubomirsky, who has been studying happiness for 18 years, says that "rumination is a huge barrier for happiness. My studies have shown that people who ruminate aren't gaining insight; they're just making themselves unhappier."[9]

When we understand the source and triggers of our anger, we can choose a different path before issues escalate. For example, not engaging can be a valuable tool in preventing the onset of anger. By learning to spot the emotional trap, we can avoid being a participant.

Consider this example: Maria receives an e-mail from her ex-husband accusing her of being irresponsible by leaving the child with a babysitter and going out. In the angry scenario, she has a huge reaction and tells him: "I hardly go out! You are the one who has all the free time to go out whenever you want! How dare you call me irresponsible! I need a break sometimes too. I don't think it's unreasonable for me to go out once a week, and my babysitter is very responsible and loves him. You are the one who is irresponsible and you know exactly why!"

Let's rethink it. What if she did not respond at all and simply went out and had a good time? Or said: "You need not worry; he is well cared for." The key to responding without anger is to give the reasonable answer regardless of whatever inflammatory thing was said to you. By doing this, you're taking the high ground, acting as though you've done nothing wrong, as though there is no need to defend yourself. (Which, by the way, is true!) Stay detached and calm. I know it's very difficult, but sometimes the best thing to do is to simply refuse to participate. Let me repeat that: *refuse to participate*!

You can practice this with strangers who get angry over nothing. Try to not to engage; do not participate. Either ignore them or respond in a nonengaging way. As the Buddhists say, "Observe without reacting."

Knowing and understanding ourselves, our past and triggers can solve some anger issues, as we've discussed. At times, however, the key to not being angry might be even more difficult. It might require not only a deep understanding of the self, but also a deep understanding of the other. This is a great challenge, especially regarding someone who might have harmed you. Many of you might ask, "why should I understand the other person, especially if they are abusive or otherwise wrong?" Let me give you an example. A boy is raised by an alcoholic father who abuses him. He then grows up troubled and has a child which he now abuses. By understanding that his propensity to abuse came from his childhood, this can remove your anger at him. Thus, understanding the underlying source of others people's thoughts and actions, can help dissipate your anger.

Does understanding the abuser mean we should accept for this child to be abused? Or do nothing about it? Absolutely not!! There is nothing that saddens me more than seeing grown men use their physical superiority to intimidate women and children instead of using it for good purposes. Understanding something does not mean accepting it. We can refuse to accept it and still act. But now we would be acting with wisdom, with a full understanding of the situation, instead of anger.

Let me share a story with you that helped me tremendously.

On one occasion, the Buddha was invited by the Brahmin Bharadvaja for alms to his house. As invited, the Buddha visited the house of the Brahmin. Instead of entertaining him, the Brahmin poured forth a torrent of abuse with the filthiest of words. The Buddha politely inquired:

"Do visitors come to your house, good Brahmin?"

"Yes," he replied.

"What do you do when they come?"

"Oh, we prepare a sumptuous feast."

"What do you if they refuse to receive the meal?"

"Why, we gladly partake of them ourselves."

"Well, good Brahmin, you have invited me for alms and entertained me with abuse which I decline to accept. So now it belongs to you."

The Buddha did not get angry or retaliate but politely gave back what the Brahmin had given him.[10]

Write down what you are angry about, and then try to find a way to understand its source. Vigorous exercise can help your mind be clearer for thought and reflection, as can a friend, meditation, and books, like the book *Mindsight* by Dr. Dan Siegel. What will it bring you to stay angry forever? How many more years of your life will you spend being filled with angry feelings? This is taking up a lot of space in your life!

Once you figure the source of your anger, it will dissipate. Then, as difficult as it may be, try to find the source of other's behaviors.

> "Holding on to anger is like grasping a hot coal with the intent of throwing it at someone else; you are the one who gets burned."
>
> —Buddha[11]

Understand the source of their actions. You need not accept their behavior. But by not getting angry, you will be acting with more wisdom about the situation.

Symbolically, you can let go of all this anger with a ritual of some kind. Maybe by throwing something heavy in a lake or flushing something down the toilet!

Cost: Free. Result: Priceless.

CHAPTER 4
"I Feel Guilty"

Looking back at my youth, there were so many instances when I felt guilty for things I shouldn't have. This continued into my adulthood. I was apologetic in my style of speaking. The manner in which I said "excuse me" to passers-by even seemed laced with guilt.

I suspect that many women are trained from birth to feel guilty by educators, family, and others. We are taught to be "nice." If someone wrongs us, we are encouraged to put ourselves in their shoes, and simply excuse their behavior. This inevitably leads us to assuming responsibility for the situation—pile on the guilt!

It's even worse for single mothers. We're supposed to feel guilty that our children are in a divorced or single-parent family; that they don't have a male father figure or not enough of one; that we are not buying them the best stuff; that we don't have enough time to put in a full day's work and taxi our kids to every activity, and look after our parents, and . . .

Is this true? Is everything your fault? I doubt it! What about the reverse? Are you taking credit for all the good you create? I doubt that too! Far from feeling guilty about your situation, why not consider the possibility that your children might be better off in a single-parent home?

Let's take the case of Rachel (not her real name), who has been the single mother of her two sons since they were 12 and 5. Now both fully grown, the kids have great personalities, work hard, and are successful students, responsible, respectful, and balanced. Rachel is hardworking, solid, and never complains. They live a "normal" middle-class life, and I respect Rachel tremendously for her strength and self-confidence in dealing with her circumstances. She kicked out her cocaine-using husband and took charge of her life and her children's future. When I ask her how she thinks her kids would have turned out had she stayed with the father, she answers: "It would've been a disaster." And how do the boys feel about being raised without a father present in their lives? "It was my older son that more or less gave me the red light to leave. I was doing the dishes one night and he said 'You know, Mom. You don't deserve all this shit from Dad. You've got to do something about this.' A month later I was out of there ... [my son] gave me a lot of strength," said Rachel.

Studies support Rachel's family experience and confirm that children of single mothers can benefit from a divorce that separates embattled parents and look forward to a bright future. The research is certainly coming out slowly, and some might call it controversial, but these are real studies that happen to match my own experience and beliefs.

A major review of more than 200 British research studies on the impact of separation and divorce on children found that although children might go though some difficult period in a divorce situation, "most children settle into a pattern of normal development."[12]

Nancy Dowd, in her book *In Defense of Single Parent Families*, states: "The commonplace assumption that single parent families are dysfunctional and bad because of inherent, fatal flaws in their structure is unsupported rhetoric. To the contrary, all we know about families indicates that structure does not dictate family function or success. Children need love, care and parenting; structure neither precludes nor insures that those things will be present."[13]

In 1994, a huge nationwide study began, involving 90,000 adolescents and their parents. Known as the National Longitudinal Study of Adolescent Health, it looked at how families and social contexts influence teen behavior and health, and their likelihood of engaging in risky behavior such as drinking, using drugs, smoking, and having early sex.[14] R. W. Blum and his colleagues examined what people often think predicts adolescent behaviors, namely: race/ethnicity, family income, and family structure. It turns out that these are actually very weak predictors. "Controlling for gender, race/ethnicity, income and family structure together explained no more than 10% of the variance in each of the 5 risky behaviors among young adolescents and no more than 7% among older youths."[15] In fact, studies show that "the one most consistently protective factor found was the presence of a positive parent-family relationship."[16] Thus, as I understand the research, and what I believe intuitively, being connected, close, and attached is more important than whether the child is in a single-parent family.

Dr. Michael Resnick, Professor of Public Health and Pediatrics at the University of Minnesota, said of his findings from the National Longitudinal Study: "So we found, for example, that young people who indicated that strong sense of bonding, that closeness and attachment to family, regardless of the nature of the family—single parent, dual parent, adoptive family—whether these kids were rich or poor and so on and so forth. These kids did better. Emotionally they were less likely to smoke cigarettes, marijuana, to use alcohol. They were less likely to attempt suicide, less likely to initiate sex at an early age. This is the world according to the adolescent."[17] In other words, it seems to be less "risky" for a child to be with a single parent who has a good bond with the child than in a two-parent family where there is no such connectedness.

If you worry about academics, then consider this study: Research scientists from Cornell University studying 13- and 14-year-old children have found that children from single-parent homes fair as well in school as those from traditional two-parent homes. A parent's marital status has little to do with how children do in academic studies.[18] "Over all, we find little or no evidence of systematic negative effects of single parenthood on children, regardless of how long they have lived with a single parent during the previous six years," says Henry Ricciuti, who is professor emeritus of human development in the College of Human Ecology at Cornell.[19] "The findings suggest that in the presence of favorable maternal characteristics, such as education and positive child expectations, along with social resources supportive of parenting, single parenthood in and of itself need not to be a risk factor for a child's performance in mathematics, reading or vocabulary or for behavior problems," Ricciuti says.[20]

These same children had been studied when they were six and seven years old, in 1999. At that time, it was found that single parenthood had no effect on their readiness for school or on their social or behavioral problems.[21]

Finally, E. Mavis Hetherington's three-decade-long study of almost 1,400 families and more than 2,500 children, *For Better or For Worse: Divorce Reconsidered* (2002), found that the great majority of children from divorced homes are "coping reasonably well and functioning in the normal range" and "go on to have reasonably happy or sometimes very happy lives."[22]

Many single mothers would not be surprised to learn that some studies have shown that children of single mothers have better communication skills. Let's not forget that Barack Obama, the 44th president of the United States, is the son of a single mother.

Children of single parents are often very close to their moms, who do not have to divide their attention between other adults in the home. There is a myth that a single mother does not have as much time to take care of her children as a married mother. Research conducted by the University of Maryland published in December 2008 puts a dent in this myth. The study measured the amount and quality of time that single mothers spend taking care of their children and found it to be almost equal to that of married mothers (83–93%). "We were surprised that these women managed to pull it off so well, often working long hours with little help, yet devoting up to 90 percent of the time to their children that married women do," says Sarah Kendig, the principal researcher.[23]

What becomes very clear from many studies is that the environment you create in your single-parent home is critical, and perhaps even more so than the divorce itself. And the relationship of the parent with the child is crucial to the well-being of the child. Your ability to recover and move toward creating a better home is the crucial first step.

I can't speak for everyone, but I'm convinced that my son will grow up happier, stronger, more peaceful, and better balanced than if his father and I had continued to live together. This doesn't mean that I think that it's better for my son to be in a single-parent home than in a two-parent home. It just means I think it's better for my son to be in a single-parent home than the *actual* two-parent home he would have had if his father and I had remained married. Children in intact homes where there is high conflict do not fair well. Had his father and I stayed in the same home, there would certainly have been conflict detrimental to my son's well-being. I really value peace, and now there is peace in my home.

So I say: "Refuse to feel guilty!" I refuse. I didn't expect or anticipate the problems I had in my marriage. I'm doing my best, trying hard, not feeling guilty. I am a good mother and a decent human being, even with my defects.

We have to be especially careful as single mothers not to end up making bad discipline decisions based on our guilt. For example, don't assume that every time your child does something inappropriate, it is related to being in a single-parent home. Consider that it just might

DO YOU KNOW WHO ELSE WAS RAISED BY A SINGLE MOTHER OR IN A FATHERLESS HOME?

Alexander Hamilton—President Gen. George Washington—President Thomas Jefferson—President James Monroe—President Andrew Jackson—President Andrew Johnson—President Rutherford B. Hayes—President Herbert Hoover—President Grover Cleveland—President Gerald Ford—President William Jefferson Clinton—President Barack Obama—U.S. Supreme Court Justice James Wilson—U.S. Supreme Court Justice John Rutledge—John Hancock—U.S. Supreme Court Justice Stephen Johnson Field—U.S. Supreme Court Justice Thomas Todd—U.S. Supreme Court Justice David Davis—U.S. Supreme Court Justice John McKinley—U.S. Supreme Court Ch. Justice (and U.S. Treasury Secretary) Salmon P. Chase—U.S. Supreme Court Justice Melville Fuller—U.S. Supreme Court Ch. Justice Edward D. White—U.S. Supreme Court Justice Benjamin N. Cardozo—U.S. Supreme Court Justice William O. Douglas—U.S. Supreme Court Justice James F. Byrnes—U.S. Supreme Court Justice Arthur J. Goldberg—U.S. Supreme Court Justice Clarence Thomas—Frederick Douglass—Gen. Robert E. Lee—Booker T. Washington—Benjamin Rush—Stephen Colbert—George Mason—Fr. Gen. Marquis de Lafayette—U.S. Senator Henry Clay—William Tecumseh Sherman—Meriwether Lewis—Eleanor Roosevelt—Jackie Robinson—Mark Twain—George Washington Carver—Nathaniel Hawthorne—Eli Whitney Jr.—U.S. House Majority Leader Steny Hamilton Hoyer—Michael Phelps—Linus Carl Pauling—Aristotle—Nicolas Copernicus—Sir Isaac Newton—Mahatma Gandhi—Leonardo da Vinci—Confucius—Jesus of Nazareth—Queen Elizabeth I—Jean-Jacques Rousseau—William Blackstone—Annie Mansfield Sullivan—Alexander Fleming—Nelson Mandela—Catherine the Great of Russia—Robert Frost—Langston Hughes—Alexandre Dumas—Gen. Alexander Haig—Alabama Governor Bibb Graves—New York Governor Al Smith—Tennessee Governor Sam Houston—Indiana Supreme Court Justice William Allen Woods—U.S. Senator Al Sharpton—U.S. Senator Robert C. "Bob" Smith—U.S. Senator John Ensign—U.S. Senator Bella Abzug—U.S. Senator William Warren "Bill" Bradley—U.S. Senator Daniel Patrick Moynihan—Queen Victoria of Britain—Alan Greenspan—Plato—Alessandro Volta—Jim Clark—Ada Lovelace—Jane Austen—George Eastman—Rosa Parks—Roy Wilson Howard—Washington State Senator Paull Shin—Johann Sebastian Bach—Gottfried Wilhelm von Leibniz—Lance

Armstrong—John Lennon—Hans Christian Andersen—Edward Jenner—Giacomo Puccini—Joseph John ("J.J.") Thomson—Bertrand Russell—Hermann Rorschach—Herman Melville—John Keats—Marian Anderson—Garry Kasparov—Sylvia Plath—Leo Tolstoy—Peyton Rous—Benjamin Carson—Raphael—David Hume—Hannah Arendt—Ralph Waldo Emerson—Stephen Crane —Friedrich Nietzsche—Agatha Christie—William Wordsworth— Max Weber—Cleopatra—Jesse Jackson—Audie Murphy—Gustav Theodor Fechner—Edgar Allen Poe—Emile Zola—William Smith —Gerald Bull—Willa Cather—Ritchie Valens—Daniel Dennett— Cass Gilbert—Mary Leakey—Joseph Stalin—Charlie Chaplin— Nelly Bly—Henry Morton Stanley—Max Born—Sarah Breedlove —Friedrich Froebel—Steve Allen—Louis Armstrong—Warren Hastings—Allan Pinkerton—Billie Holiday—Hank Williams—Malcolm X—Carol Burnett—Thomas Green Clemson—John Irving— J. R. R. Tolkien—Charles Bronson—Tom Blake—Paulette Goddard—Gene Hackman—Robert Hooke—James Byron Dean—Halle Berry—Benjamin Bratt—Eddie Murphy—Caroline Kennedy Schlossberg—Deborah Sampson—Ralph Ellison—California Supreme Court Justice Rose Bird—Eric Clapton—Eamon de Valera—William Reddington Hewlett—J. Marvin Herndon— Mother Angelica—Karl Rove—Julius Caesar—Muhammed—Massachusetts Gov. Deval Patrick—F. Whitten Peters—Henry Talbot —Arthur C. Clarke—Jim Rogan—Frederick W. Alt—Emil J. Freireich—Willie Nelson—Charlotte Perkins Gilman—Victor Herbert —Bessie Coleman—Dorothy Andersen—Chiang Kai-shek—Vidal Sassoon—Coco Chanel—Anderson Hayes Cooper—James Brown —Kenneth Grahame—Hunter "Patch" Adams—Jack Nicholson— Roald Dahl—William Lloyd Garrison—Douglas Fairbanks—David Harker—Robert Fulton—Irving Berlin—Jonathan Swift—Peggy Drexler—Art Buchwald—Carolyn Jones—Doris Roberts—Loretta Young—Marilyn Monroe—Barbara Stanwick—Steve McQueen— Cher—Pierce Brosnan—Wayne Dyer—Francis Alice Kellor— Sophia Loren—Stephen King—Sir Charles Bell—Whoopi Goldberg—Richard Wright—Percy Spencer—Ward Connerly—Fatty Arbuckle—Katherine Burr Blodgett—Dorothea Lange—Frances Kellor—Gloria Steinem—Gloria Gaynor—Jon Stewart—Bette Davis—Audrey Hepburn—Tom Cruise—Bill Cosby—Barry White —Susanna Harding—Jodie Foster—Patsy Cline—Ed Bradley— Tom Monaghan—Rickey Henderson . . . and many many more.

Source: http://singlemomprofessor.blogspot.com/2009_01_01_archive.html; http://www.thelizlibrary.org/fatherless/effects-of-fatherlessness.html.

be the typical attempt of a child to get what he likes having nothing to do with your marital status.

Assuming that your child must be traumatized can become a self-fulfilling prophecy because the child is being treated as such. I suggest removing this possibility unless there is a clear link. Your child may actually be fine and "normal." Don't forget that many children in two-parent families live with all kinds of difficulties in their child-hoods as well and still turn out OK.

Another important consequence of walking around with guilt on your shoulders is that it can make your child think you did something really wrong—that everything is your fault. Why else would you be acting so apologetic and "guilty"?

When I feel bad about something, if I was impatient with my son one day, for example, I try to remind myself of the good things I did that day for him. I remember that I read him a book in the morning; played a tickle game in the car; worked to make a living to support us; took his friend over to our house; cooked dinner; put cream on his boo-boo . . .

CAN DIVORCE ACTUALLY IMPROVE YOUR RELATIONSHIP WITH YOUR CHILDREN?

Single moms often depend on daughters for support and cooperation after a divorce, but is this necessarily negative? Joyce Arditti, Ph.D., of the Virginia Polytechnic Institute studied 58 young adults and their relationship with their divorced mothers. She found that "moms leaning on their children for emotional support and advice contrib-uted to a sense of equality, closeness and friend status. These values seemed to be valued by the participants in this study."

The interviews indicate that their relationships are based on **friendship not hierarchy**. Although these parent-child relationships are different, they are not necessarily more difficult, says Arditti, who adds: "Using your child as a confidante is not necessarily wrong. And it actually may set up opportunities for children to talk to mothers."

Source: Joyce A. Arditti, "Rethinking Relationships between Divorced Mothers and Their Children: Capitalizing on Family Strengths," *Family Relations* 48, no. 2 (April 1999): 109–19, http://www.jstor.org/pss/585074. Last accessed March 18, 2010; Holly Parker, "The Upside of Divorce," *Psychology Today*, September 1, 1999, http://www.psychologytoday.com/articles/pto -19990901-000014.html. Last accessed March 18, 2010.

all this in a typical day. My mistakes surely cannot erase everything good that I do. Let us not forget about all that we do as mothers.

Keep in mind: If you feel guilty, your kids will think everything is your fault.

It's time to stop feeling guilty. I'm sure things are not completely your fault, and if they were partly, then let it go because you are human. Focus on what you do well, on all the time and effort you dedicate to your children, and on all the good you do for others. I have no doubt all that outweighs your imperfections. No one is perfect. The trick is to simply take what you have and to make the best of it. There is an old Jewish proverb that says, "G-d could not be everywhere and therefore he made mothers."

Try this exercise to rid yourself of guilt. Buy a Guilt Journal and write down the things you feel guilty about. Make an action plan to get rid of these ASAP! As a friend of mine who passed away at age 32 of multiple sclerosis used to say, "Just kick the guilt away. Just kick it away!!!"

CHAPTER 5

"Things Are Awful"

Two months after the separation with my then husband, my eyes still red from crying, I went to a child's birthday party. I was still pretty shaken up. Seeing all the people there in so-called "normal" families, while I was alone with my son, added to the awkwardness. I ran into someone I knew who had divorced several years earlier. Hoping for some encouragement from a fellow single mother, I asked "Will this get better?" Her answer: "Well, I would never wish this on anyone." Ouch!

Although I like this person very much and continue to respect her, I decided that I would not allow myself to accept such a negative fate.

Now that I have adopted a positive approach to life, I realize the harmful effects of *negative speak*. Oh yes . . . I am still bombarded with negative words and concepts about single motherhood. I simply refuse to allow them to influence my world.

And those thoughts don't always come from others. Half the battle is paying attention to how you explain events to yourself. A person's explanatory style greatly affects attitude. There's a big difference between saying "I'm having a bad day" and "Life sucks." There's a big difference between thinking "I didn't speak nicely to my son this morning when he spilled cereal" and "I'm a terrible mother."

Yale University researcher Becca Levy, Ph.D., and her colleagues, conduct research to test how words and perceptions can directly affect people. In one study, 660 individuals aged 50 and older were asked about their perceptions of aging. Incredibly, those with more positive self-perceptions of aging, (which was assessed 23 years earlier) lived 7.5 years longer than those with who had a more negative perception.[24]

In other words, self-perceptions can be so powerful, that it can affect longevity.

I suggest that seeing single motherhood negativity can have a harmful effect on us. So instead of associating single mothers with words like: *helpless*, *weak*, *tired*, *desperate*, *unstable*, and *incapable*, I suggest focusing on the fact that single mothers are RESPONSIBLE, STRONG, EMPATHETIC, HARDWORKING, RESOURCEFUL, COURAGEOUS, ADMIRABLE, and SIMPLY AMAZING!

Is it unrealistic to be positive? Am I ignoring reality? I don't think so. There truly are positive sides to being a single mother. One of them is that we are no longer living in an unhealthy marriage or couple! I have asked every woman I have ever spoken to who is separated or divorced whether she wished to go back to her previous life. Most of the time, the answer is "No." Occasionally I hear, "maybe I would *if only* ... " Then I'd ask whether they would go back to the relationship "exactly as it was," without the hypotheticals. The answer is always "No way!" So for many single mothers, the experience of single motherhood is actually an improvement on their lives. Is it unrealistic to see being a single mother in this way? I don't think so, and that's not a rose-colored view. It is our reality.

If you are a single mother due to separation or divorce, it is probably for a reason. You might like to pretend that the relationship was fine, but if it had all been fine, then it probably wouldn't have ended. For many of us, the reality is that either we were incompatible with our partners, someone was unhappy in the relationship, or some other irreparable situation occurred. In too many cases, there was a lot of conflict, verbal abuse, physical abuse, or the threat of it.

I know that whatever challenges I face now, I am better off. I know I am not alone and that many other single mothers are capable of seeing the positive aspect of what they experienced. When surfing blogs and message boards for signs of positive attitudes about single motherhood, I discovered that there are many women who have similar attitudes, and this is inspiring to all of us. A compilation of their statements are in Section 6. I invite you to look through a few of them every night to remind yourself of some of the "positive reality" that you are undoubtedly experiencing as well.

You are not doomed to a miserable life because of this experience. Research shows that even the most difficult experiences in life often change people for the better. Studies of people who have experienced horrific events indicate that only a few actually become seriously troubled into adulthood. Many if not most people get stronger, grow, and even thrive in the wake of difficulties, a condition known as "post-traumatic growth." And you can too!

So, it's time to adopt a new attitude. Yes, you are a single mother, but you are not alone. In the United States and Canada there are more than 90 million mothers, and given the current divorce rate, a great number of them will experience single motherhood at some point in their lives. As single mom Liz (not her real name) puts it: "Either your glass is half full or half empty . . . If you constantly consider and focus on 'what's the positive thing that happened today,' rather than the negative, you're going to come out of this in a lot better shape." I couldn't agree more! Let's just say goodbye to *negative speak*!

CHAPTER 6

"I'm So Worried"

We all tend to put off living. We have dreams about something over the horizon, instead of enjoying what we have today. We worry and miss out on the daily gifts of life. Worrying about the future doesn't allow you to enjoy the present. As Albert Einstein said, "I never think of the future—it comes soon enough."

Does this mean we shouldn't make any plans about the future? No. Absolutely not! We can prepare for tomorrow. But the idea is not to carry around "anxiety" for tomorrow. Think about everything you've worried about in the past few years. How many of them have really happened? Ninety-nine percent of things we worry about don't happen, so we have wasted a lot of time worrying for nothing!

One way to put life in perspective is to not make snap judgments until you have the whole story. Before worrying, panicking, or forming an opinion about something, get the *facts*. If you don't have the time to get the facts, then reserve your opinion until you have some. For example, many parents worry about child abductions. The media plays on our fear to get our attention. An article by Maia Szalavitz shows how the media can give misleading impressions. She reviewed comments in the media, where it was reported that there are 5,000 American children that go missing each year in nonfamily abductions, giving the impression that there are 5,000 horrific kidnappings by a stranger or acquaintance. In fact, she says, "According to the Justice Department, there are only about 115 such incidents each year."[25] The rest fall into other categories, such as teenagers running away with friends and romantic partners, and other situations. I am not trying to belittle the horrific nature of these 115, just trying to show how getting the facts is important.

We can also reduce worry by understanding risks and statistics. Most of us were not taught statistics, and when we don't understand statistics, politicians, businesses, and shallow or careless news stories have an easier time manipulating us. The resulting anxieties can seriously damage our health and well-being.

If you want to make informed decisions, make an effort to understand statistics. I read an interesting article in *Scientific American Mind* about statistical manipulation and the important difference between *absolute* risk and *relative* risks.

In the article, they discussed the warning given by the UK Committee on Safety of Medicines about the *twofold* increase of life threatening blood clots from the use of certain contraceptive pills. That's a 100 percent increase! The committee notified the media, doctors, pharmacists, and directors of public health. Because the data was reported in this way, many women panicked and stopped taking the pill as a result. This led to 800 more pregnancies of girls under 16 and about 13,000 additional abortions in the following years. A more straightforward manner of reporting the data might have led to different results. The authors in the article explain the difference between reporting a relative risk and an absolute risk. The risk of blood clots did *double* in the third-generation pill (*relative* risk). But because the risk was 1 in 7,000 women, the increase made it 2 in 7,000 (*absolute* risk).[26]

Absolute risks are typically smaller numbers. This is why careless news reporting allows for headlines in terms of *relative* risk. "Increases the risk from 1 in 7,000, to 2 in 7,000" becomes "**Doubling** the risk of blood clots."

Think about this next time someone feeds you with some information that has statistics. Think about this next time someone says something like, "There has been a 50 percent increase in theft in the area." What does that translate to in terms of absolute risk? Try to get the real facts. Once you have the facts, then you can make a decision of what to do about the situation, including deciding to do nothing. Any time spent worrying after that won't help in any way.

Here's another perfect example, this time about single parenting. Dennis Saleebey, in *Strengths Perspective in Social Work Practice*, writes about the expected adverse outcomes in children (psychological, behavioral, social, and academic) as a result of living in single-parent homes. He discussed a study that concluded that children in single-parent homes have **twice the risk** for developing a psychiatric illness, killing themselves or attempting suicide, and developing an alcohol-related disorder (relative risk). He also explains how the presentation of this statistic by the media can affect our perception:

> For example, a recent rigorous study comparing children in single and two-parent households in Sweden did indeed find the former at roughly twice the risk for developing a psychiatric illness, killing themselves or attempting suicide, and developing an alcohol-related disorder (Weitoft et al., 2003). This study was highly publicized in newspapers across the country in headlines such as "One Parent, Twice the Trouble" (Ross, 2003). However, what was not addressed either by the researchers or the reporters were the actual numbers or percentages of youth with adverse outcomes. Upon examining the tables in the actual study, one finds that only 2% of the girls and 1.5% of the boys from single-parent families developed psychiatric problems as children and adolescents and only .9% and .7% as young adults. This is indeed twice the adversity than that experienced by individuals growing up in a two parent household. However, the untold story is that 98% of children and adolescents in single-parent families did *not* have psychiatric disorders. Similarly, 98% of the girls and 99% of the boys did *not* commit suicide; 99% of the girls and 98.8% of the boys did *not* commit a violent act; 99% of the girls and 98.8% of the boys did *not* develop an alcohol-related disorder, and so on (Weitoft et al., 2003).[27]

Aside from the getting the facts, another useful method to combat worry is to engage in something that requires thinking about something else. It's hard to worry when you are doing something constructive. Doing a routine task might not do the trick since your mind will still be free to worry while doing it. Try instead to do an activity that requires your full engagement. Find something that stops your mind chatter. Lose yourself in something. Use your skills in something you like. It also helps to get involved in other people's lives and problems. Helping others will take your mind off yourself and your own problems. Basically, you need to get yourself busy and thinking about something or someone else to help alleviate your worries.

You should be enjoying your time after work, and especially the moments after the kids go to sleep. What a waste to spend it worrying about endless details, magnifying all issues and imagining all the millions of possibilities of every single eventuality. French philosopher

Montaigne said of his own life, "My life has been full of terrible misfortunes most of which never happened."[28]

Make a list of things you *can* do when worry creeps in. When you see it coming, then you can use one of your tactics. And remember what Shantideva wrote: "If you can solve your problem, then what is the need of worrying? If you cannot solve it, then what is the use of worrying?"[29]

CHAPTER 7

"I Have Low Self-Esteem"

Our tendency as mothers is to be acutely aware of our children's self-esteem. We are quick to praise them and to help them like, respect, and value themselves. But what about our own self-esteem? Have you thought about your self-esteem lately? How do you feel about yourself? Self-esteem has been shown to be directly connected with happiness,[30] so improving your self-esteem is an important step toward improving your life.

I have always been impressed by the courage and selflessness in every single mother I've met. But my praise of single mothers is *not* going to raise your self-esteem. Standing in front of the mirror repeating phrases that are supposed to improve your self-esteem won't help either. Psychologists Joanne Wood and John Lee from the University of Waterloo in Ontario and Elaine Perunovic from the University of New Brunswick found that using overly positive praise such as "I am a loveable person" or "I will succeed" made individuals with low self-esteem feel even *worse*.[31] "The psychologists suggested that, like overly positive praise, unreasonably positive self-statements, such as 'I accept myself completely,' can provoke contradictory thoughts in individuals with low self-esteem. Such negative thoughts can overwhelm the positive thoughts. And, if people are instructed to focus exclusively on positive thoughts, they may find negative thoughts to be especially discouraging."[32] This is a sure reminder of a concept you will find throughout this book: that being optimistic does *not* mean being unrealistic or unauthentic.

Before getting married, I actually thought of myself as relatively attractive, smart, strong, and full of good qualities. Over the course of my marriage, I began to doubt everything I did. I felt ugly and I cast myself as a loser. My self-esteem had never been lower. Soon after the separation, however, I began to recover my old perspective. Not that I didn't have many, many days of feeling low, but on the whole, I started to change, to feel better about myself, physically and emotionally. I did it by applying to myself the same basic principles used to teach children self-esteem since the dawn of time.

Have you ever noticed how proud children are when they succeed at something new and challenging, especially if it takes many attempts—and how unimpressed they are with themselves if someone does it for them? They feel proud because *they* tried it and *they* did it themselves. This may sound obvious, but one of the keys to building your self-esteem is to actually feel proud of yourself. And the key to doing this is to do things that you feel proud of. This may be different for different people. But a good way to practice this is to do things that may be slightly out of your comfort zone.

> "Be daring; be first; be different, be just."
>
> —Anita Roddick[33]

Does that mean you should go skydiving? Not necessarily. The idea is to try to do things that are a little challenging or new to you, but not necessarily terrifying. Even if you fail, you will feel proud of yourself for coping with your fear of failure. In fact, if you fail several times before succeeding, your self-esteem will likely rise even higher.

The habit of doing things out of your comfort zone—and I say *habit* because you should do this regularly—will also help to dissipate your fears in general, because you will be in the habit of doing things that are slightly scary. You will get comfortable being a bit daring.

I regularly do things that are slightly out of my comfort zone; in fact, I do them on purpose. They could even be silly things, but I use them as opportunities to make me feel good about myself. For example, I went to another city for work and while walking around a mall, I noticed an indoor amusement park with a huge roller coaster. I'm not usually afraid of roller coasters but I was slightly afraid of this one. I decided to buy a ticket precisely *because* I was a bit afraid. I went on that roller coaster, by myself, surrounded by cars full of screaming happy children. When I got off, I felt great! Sounds silly? Well, try it and you'll see!

Of course, you don't need to do something as dramatic as riding roller coasters. Everyone has their own comfort level. The key is to recognize yours, then challenge yourself a bit at a time. Maybe there are other things you would like to do but are slightly hesitant about doing—perhaps smiling at someone at a coffee shop, telling your child's teacher what you really think, submitting a book proposal,

"If you hear a voice within you say 'you cannot paint,' then by all means paint, and that voice will be silenced."

—Vincent Van Gogh[34]

or Rollerblading. It may be as gentle as learning a new language or singing karaoke. If you do things you are slightly afraid of doing, you will feel good about yourself because even if you don't conquer the thing itself, you have conquered the fear of trying it.

Twice a week I go to my all-male martial arts class. It makes me physically stronger but more importantly, it makes me mentally strong because it takes all the guts I have to go there. When people ask me why I do martial arts, I always answer "mostly to strengthen my mind." Aside from the physical benefits, it trains me to face challenges in a cool and calm way and to look challenges and fear in the eye. I feel exhausted, overwhelmed, yet proud of myself every time I leave that class.

Don't be afraid of failures, as long as you learn from them. The most successful scientists are also the ones who failed the most. Let's redefine what it means to succeed and what it means to fail. Most people assume that there is failure on one side and success on the other. And they are trying to get to the success side:

Failure ← **YOU** → Success.

But in fact, failure is a stepping stone toward success! It's along the path. It need not be avoided, but actually *experienced* in order to get to success. It's on the way there:

YOU → Failure → Failure → Success.

When you do try something new, keep in mind that success is relative. I realized this when I entered a distance run at age 38. At the start line were all types of very fit bodies clearly experienced in running. As a joke, I told one of the people I knew that he had an unfair advantage over me since he was not carrying the extra weight I had on my body. For things to be fair, I joked, he should put a 30-pound backpack over his shoulders for the run. But as I started running, I realized the truth of what I was saying. In this race, there were people who were geneti-cally better equipped to run, some who had the time and money to train better, some who were older and some younger, others who had psychological traumas from childhood that might affect their abil-ities to motivate themselves, others who might have previous leg inju-ries, and others with little training, a bit overweight, and lacking experience (me).

I realized that success and "winning" is relative to *yourself*. The only person you need to challenge and beat is yourself in order to raise self-esteem. I saw a much older woman running at my slow pace and I real-ized that her self-esteem, upon completing this run, would surely be raised, as much as, if not more, than the person who actually comes in first place (who might have won many races before). So I happily continued, with no concern but my own achievement, which would be to simply finish this difficult challenge, and I did!!! I came in *last place* according to the stopwatches. When I arrived, there were only a few people left at the finish line because the whole crowd had already dispersed much earlier. There weren't even any snacks left when I got there—they had already packed them up. But in my mind I was floating in achievement because I beat my previous self, who was never able to jog for more than 10 minutes just two years earlier.

This is the way I think we should approach all challenges. Forget what others have done or can do. Your challenge is to improve *yourself*. If it has always been hard for you to smile at a stranger and you do it, then this is success! If it has been hard for you to exercise and you man-age to do a 15-minute power walk, then this is success! If you are always negative and you manage to see things more positively for a full day, this is success. If you were always giving in to fear and you were able to do something despite this feeling, this is a huge achievement!

Try to find something that can help you focus on yourself and raise your self-esteem. Get in the habit of spotting "out-of-comfort-zone" actions. Write them down, and then start doing them. Find new opportunities for feeling good about yourself.

Let me end this chapter with a fun fact. Did you know single moms have larger brains? Well, they do! At least the carnivores that John Gittleman, a University of Tennessee zoologist, studied do. He com-pared raccoons, ursids, felids, and other mothers who receive no help from mates or other females, with those that do receive parenting help. He found that "carnivorous females with solitary mothering habits have larger brains in proportion to their body size than female carnivores who obtain parenting help from mates or other community members." These mothers spend 80 percent of their time taking care of their young, doing everything from finding a den and food to teaching their young to hunt and protecting them from predators.[35]

Given a solitary mother's need to be so perceptive, deal with so much information, and multitask, this seems to make sense to me!

CHAPTER 8

"No One Respects Me"

I know I am not alone in having walked around feeling that no one respects me. I am sure that I am not alone in having been yelled at, insulted, or taken for granted.

Lana (not her real name) is a young Filipino woman I spoke to once about becoming a live-in caregiver in Canada. Canada has a program where nannies or caregivers can be sponsored by Canadians to come and live with them while taking care of their children or the elderly. After two years, these caregivers can apply to get the Canadian equivalent of a Green Card. According to the rules of the game, these caregivers, often from countries like the Philippines, are paid a certain wage and are supposed to be paid overtime. Lana told me stories of how employers often abuse these women by requiring them to work extra hours unpaid (slavery by any definition). The women are often afraid to speak up. Although technically they can change employers and continue with someone else to complete the two-year requirement, it is not an easy thing to do. They may fear not finding another employer and often endure unfair treatment for the sake of getting their papers.

But this 90-pound Filipino girl, Lana, whom I so admire, told me that when she got to Canada, her employer wanted her to work extra hours with no pay. So she asked the employer, "How would you feel if we reversed the situation? If I were the employer and you were the caregiver and I wanted *you* to work for free?" She did this without anger or hostility, and she described to me how the employer's jaw dropped at the realization.

She ended up changing employers and found another job with a more considerate family. She told me that she really disliked people abusing her. She thinks she should be treated with the same consideration she gives employers. She also told me that she likes to tell other Filipino women a simple sentence: "If they abuse you, it's because you allow yourself to be abused."

I do not want to oversimplify the issue of abuse or respect, but certainly, at least in North America, there are *some* things we can do to stop people from disrespecting or abusing us. This isn't about blaming the victim, but empowering us to put limits or boundaries on what we accept. If this tiny, uprooted Filipino girl can stand up to disrespectful treatment, then so can we! If someone acts disrespectfully, we can leave the situation, hang up the phone, get help, or refuse to engage.

The basis of getting respect is having self-respect. Let me repeat that. *The basis of getting respect is having self-respect.* And you do not have to be angry or tough to have self-respect. You just have to feel it.

This brings to mind a little tale about the concept of respect. I remember working in a firm with a colleague who was respected by the group due to his position and title. I did not share this feeling. I did not admire him professionally nor did I admire the manner in which he treated others. And why should I have? Does having a title, money, or a nice suit mean you deserve respect? Does having no money, being an immigrant, or having an accent mean that you do *not* deserve any? Not in my book! I respect my kind Filipino friend with no legal status much more.

Rethink your concepts of respect. Perhaps this might make you realize that you deserve some. It is only then that others will read self-respect in your eyes. And for those who do not respect you, you will be less affected if you already have your own self-respect.

This reminds me of a driving incident not long ago. A woman stopped at her stop sign and then took off in her car and almost hit me. I had no stop sign, so she was clearly at fault. And we were now both stopped and looking at each other after braking suddenly. I pointed to her stop sign. She yelled, "So go already, you stupid b___!" I smiled and continued with my day.

> "No one, Eleanor Roosevelt said, can make you feel inferior without your consent. Never give it."
>
> —Marian Wright Edelman[36]

CHAPTER 9

"I'm Helpless"

In 1965, Martin E. P. Seligman accidentally discovered an unexpected phenomenon while doing an experiment on dogs. In the experiment, the dogs were given a harmless shock after the sound of a tone, to see whether the tone would trigger fear when the bell rang. It was along the same line as the famous Pavlov experiment that led to dogs salivating upon the ringing of a bell before receiving food.

But an interesting thing happened in the next part of Seligman's experiment. The conditioned dogs were put into a shuttle box, which had a low fence that the dogs could see over and easily jump over. Yet when the bell rang, the dogs did not jump over the fence as they were expected to! Even when shocked, the dogs still wouldn't jump over as a normal dog would have. The researchers concluded that these dogs, who had learned that attempting to escape shocks was futile in the previous experiment, no longer tried to do so. The dogs had learned to be helpless![37]

The experiment led to a scientific revolution in the psychology field, a theory called *learned helplessness*. It's a condition in which you feel powerless to help yourself due to the experience of being powerless in the past.

Think about this concept for a moment. Do you feel helpless? Where in your life did you learn that you have no control over your life? That nothing you do matters? In your family home? In your marriage? Perhaps it's time to discuss what you've experienced with someone of confidence and see if there is some connection you can make with why you are paralyzed in some area of your life today.

I will not pretend to be a psychologist able to solve all these issues. I am only offering ideas to you so you can investigate your own sources of inaction further and discover whether any of these theories apply to you. For it is only when we find these internal connections that we can break free from feelings of paralysis.

If you want to change or improve your life, you must believe that you can influence things in your life. If you believe you have no control over your life and that you are helpless, then you will not take steps toward making any changes. Let me repeat that in a different way: *if you believe you are helpless, then you cannot make any changes in your life*. It is no different from the dogs who felt there was no point jumping over the fence since they believed that they could not prevent the shocks.

There is always something we can do in any given situation. Sometimes we need to sit and think but we can always find something that is within our control. For example, one thing you can *always* do if you have been a victim in some way is to talk about it or expose it. Sometimes the only way to heal is not to "get over it" or "forget about it," but to tell someone and be listened to.

In one instance when I felt completely helpless in the face of a situation which was very difficult and that I considered highly unjust, I spend hours crying and thinking of what I can do. I could not find anything. The feeling of complete helplessness was killing me. Finally, at 3:00 am, I decided that I will do a small hunger strike as a personal protest to the injustice even if it would not change the result of the problem. When I decided to do this, my feelings of helplessness were completely alleviated, I felt happy about staying true to myself, and then I was able to come up with several constructive ideas for the problem. This was a reminder to me that there is *always* something we can do. At the most basic level (or some would say, at the most elevated level), we can always control our breathing, watch our minds, and accept the truth of the moment.

Maybe it's time to challenge your feelings of helplessness and stop the pain of those shocks, and try to make changes in the areas in your life you *do* have control over. Maybe it's time to jump over that fence! As a start, you can start adopting the 22 Happiness Strategies in the next chapter. These are all *within your control*. There is not one strategy that is not possible for you. They are yours to adopt or ignore. It's up to you!

SECTION 3

On the Road to Happiness

Once you have emptied your cup from all, or even some, of the negative emotions—anger, anxiety, fear, helplessness, guilt, worry—you will have some space. Space to fill your cup with new thoughts, ideas, and practices on how to be happier.

But first, we need to get a clear idea of what happiness actually *is* and what it isn't. Let's start by dispelling a few myths about happiness.

MYTH #1
MONEY = HAPPINESS

The average U.S. citizen's buying power has almost tripled in the last four decades. We have twice as many cars, not to mention laptops, TVs, iPods, and cell phones.[1] We have clean water at our fingertips, microwaves, food, and shelter with the ability to adjust the temperature to the exact desired degree, all of which are but a dream for many people in the world.

You'd think we'd be happier. Yet research shows we are no happier now than in the 1950s.[2] In fact, the National Institute of Mental Health estimates that an unbelievable "26.2 percent of Americans ages 18 and older—about one in four adults—suffer from a diagnosable mental disorder in a given year."[3]

Residents of Europe, Australia, and Japan do not show a significant rise in happiness levels either. Although residents of these countries are somewhat happier than people in countries with extreme poverty, the

"Focusing your life solely on making a buck shows a poverty of ambition. It asks too little of yourself. And it will leave you unfulfilled."

—Barack Obama[5]

increase of real income over the past decades has not led to increased happiness.[4]

Ironically, studies show that pursuing materialistic goals can make people quite unhappy especially their goals are for showing off or getting more power or fame as opposed to helping others. Materialistic individuals have been shown to experience depression, anxiety, narcissism, and various other problems of well-being. The more they " 'buy into' the messages of consumer society, the lower their levels of personal well-being, and the higher their levels of distress."[6] Conversely, those who strive for "intimacy, personal growth, and contribution to the community" as opposed to those who are money hungry, experience a higher quality of life.[7]

As single mom Cheryl (not her real name) points out, "You don't need as much money to have a very fulfilling life, for sure. You need to have the bare minimum. And you have to be fulfilled with your career and your life to raise your kids properly."

Research supports Cheryl's experience. Assuming basic necessities are met, income is not correlated to an increase in happiness. "Ergo," writes psychologist David Myers, "wealth is like health: Although its utter absence breeds misery, having it is no guarantee of happiness."[8]

Is this surprising? It does not surprise me much that all the increased materialism does not result in increased happiness or social well-being. Advertising constantly tries to convince us that if we buy something, we will be happy. But how could brand-name shoes bring happiness? How could having an expensive purse bring happiness? They will not. You'll have to look elsewhere for happiness.

MYTH #2
NO PROBLEMS = HAPPINESS

You might think that people seem happier than you because they have more fortunate lives or fewer "problems" than you do. But happy people do not necessarily experience more successes or fewer problems than unhappy people. Unless you are living in dire circumstances, it is not changes in your objective circumstances that will necessarily lead to enduring happiness.

Even if you achieved a dream of being rich, famous, or anything else—even if you got exactly what you wanted or "made it"—your feelings of bliss would likely only be temporary. People tend to eventually adapt to new circumstances, whether good or bad, and go right back to their usual state of emotions.[9]

This tendency to adapt is why specific life circumstances do not typically or significantly affect people's levels of happiness. Unless you are living in extreme conditions—such as a country where women are oppressed and there is no democracy—research has shown time and time again that external conditions make little difference in people's levels of happiness. Happy and unhappy people generally have the same types of life experiences and the same number of bad experiences. We all experience the regular ups and downs of life like money problems, divorces, losses, death in the family, lost jobs, etc. These experiences affect happiness only in the short term, and people tend to return to a point very close to their baseline.

As we will see, the difference between happy and unhappy people is how they *react* to circumstances and life events, rather than the existence of these objective circumstances.

As single mothers, we need to stop thinking that we are unhappy only because of a specific circumstance such as being a single mother, or because we are divorced. More importantly, we need to stop thinking that we will achieve happiness *if only* we could achieve some specific circumstance.

Consider single mom Sally's (not her real name) description of a friend in her life-coaching class: "She's married. She's living the clichéd dream. Great husband. Four kids. Huge house. Great lifestyle. They travel. The whole thing. They're really involved with their kid's school; she doesn't have to work. Whatever she does is because she wants to. And she's still on this journey of self-discovery. She still feels like she has these demons! So [having a ton of money] is still not going to be the end."

Even if you lose your 10–100 pounds, meet an amazing man, or double your income, you will not necessarily end up happier in the long run. You will likely settle into any new role and go back to your current habitual state of happiness. Even winning the lottery won't do it. A study conducted on lottery winners demonstrated that they were no happier than nonwinners. In fact, they enjoyed simple pleasures *less*.[10]

So if you are looking for happiness in a permanent way, you will not likely get it through specific life events. Then how do we increase our levels of happiness permanently? I will share some strategies with you once we dispel a few more myths.

MYTH #3
MARRIAGE = HAPPINESS

Getting married is not a guarantee of increasing happiness (as many of us already know). According to a 15-year study published in the *Journal of Personality and Social Psychology* in 2003, for most people, getting married did not translate to being more satisfied with life. The study measured the life satisfaction levels of more than 24,000 individuals living in Germany. Psychologist and lead author Richard E. Lucas, Ph.D., of Michigan State University found that "most people were no more satisfied with life after marriage than they were prior to marriage."[11] Although people might have small spikes of happiness just before and after life events like getting married, they usually get right back to the same "level of happiness" as before getting married.

The good news is that when something bad happens, we might experience some downward spikes in our levels of happiness but we will also usually bounce right back to where we were. After several years, even most widows and widowers eventually return to the similar levels of life satisfaction as they had before losing their spouses.[12]

MYTH #4
YOUTHFULNESS = HAPPINESS

Is happiness reserved for youth? Not so. We often hear stereotypes about what you are supposed to feel when you go through your "midlife crisis," "empty-nest syndrome," and old age. But according to research, you can be equally happy at any age.[13]

In fact, some research shows that people grow happier with age. With age comes wisdom and the confidence to make choices about what to pursue without feeling guilty or pressured from outside sources. This is good news for all of us.

MYTH #5
MEN ARE HAPPIER THAN WOMEN

Men and women go through different types of feelings and cope differently with their problems. And men tend to be happier with money while women find greater happiness through their relationships with their friends, children, co-workers, and bosses.

But are men happier than women or vice versa? According to an online survey conducted in 2008 by the global marketing company Nielsen on almost 30,000 people in more than 51 countries, women are happier than men in 48 of the 51 countries surveyed. Men were found to be happier only in Brazil, South Africa, and Vietnam. "Because they are happier with non-economic factors, women's happiness is more recession-proof, which might explain why women around the world are happier in general than men are," says Bruce Paul, vice president of consumer research at Nielsen.[14]

MYTH #6
PHYSICAL ATTRACTIVENESS = HAPPINESS

Many of us think that if we could only lose weight or look better, we would be happy. But research says that there is only a weak positive correlation between physically attractiveness and happiness. Sonja Lyubomirsky, in her book *The How of Happiness: A Scientific Approach to Getting the Life You Want*, elaborates on research that shows that good-looking people are not any happier. So for most people, she writes, becoming more beautiful will not make you happier. What might make a difference, however, is your self-perception, more than your objective beauty.[15]

I guess that's no big surprise. We all have "gorgeous" friends who are miserable. And we all know "ugly" people who are very happy.

If your goals are related to your beauty, you might be headed down a dangerous road—a psychological dead end! After conducting their study in 2009, three University of Rochester researchers discussed the goal of pursuing beauty: "People understand that it's important to pursue goals in their lives and they believe that attaining these goals will have positive consequences. This study shows that this is not true for all goals," says author Edward Deci, professor of psychology and the Gowen Professor in the Social Sciences at the university.[16]

Don't spend another penny on those "beauty" magazines! They will just make you feel ugly. Focus instead on having a healthy body and healthy mind and pursuing intrinsic goals, and your beauty will shine through. Everyone knows that the most attractive thing you can wear is the expression on your face. Focus your energy on things that can actually affect your happiness. Let's discuss some final myths and start to learn what actually *can* make a difference in our lives!

MYTH #7
PLEASURE = HAPPINESS

Let's not fall prey to the fake "happiness" that Hollywood bombards us with. This is more accurately described by psychologists as "pleasure." Pleasure is—a "feel good" emotion that we are often trapped into pursuing. Research has shown that focusing simply on pleasure and enjoyment will not lead to greater life satisfaction. Martin Seligman, said to be the founder of positive psychology, describes what happens when we try to take shortcuts, in his renowned book *Authentic Happiness*:

> The belief that we can rely on shortcuts to happiness, joy, rapture, comfort, and ecstasy, rather than be entitled to these feelings by the exercise of personal strengths and virtues, leads to legions of people who in the middle of great wealth are starving spiritually. Positive emotion alienated from the exercise of character leads to emptiness, to inauthenticity, to depression, and, as we age, to the gnawing realization that we are fidgeting until we die.[17]

No doubt we can all think of activities we have engaged in that might have brought instant pleasure but that did not lead to happiness, whether it's pills, sex, shopping, alcohol, or the scalpel. We've learned that these do not bring about long-term joy and well-being.

The meaningful or *eudaimonic* aspects of happiness are deeper than pleasure. They include acting in accord with or realizing one's true self and potential, acting in accordance with one's deeply held values, pursuing personal growth and development, contributing to the lives of others and trying to attain our highest human nature. A greater attention to these goals, while still enjoying some pleasures, can improve your sense of well-being.

In fact, things might be more interconnected than they first appear. Having a greater mental balance and healthy mind after examination of ourselves in Section 2 allows us to seek more meaningful goals, and even give us a greater ability to enjoy simple pleasures in our external world.

Consider Eve's story (not her real name) about how she recovered from her divorce: "I most likely probably did the quick fixes. My quick fix was always a piece of clothing, a new pair of shoes, some new makeup whatever. . . . Originally I did fill up my weekends off with lots of people. I thought OK, here's my chance to reconnect to friends or family members, and I would have lunch dates. OK, let's go to the gallery. I filled it up with people. And I started to realize that that became another responsibility and obligation that was actually stressful. And I was constantly repeating my stories, my woes, my upset. And it became tedious and I didn't like who I was being. So I actually found far more growth and solace and I fed my soul by just going out on a Saturday with absolutely no commitments or lunch dates and just did whatever I felt like. I would go downtown and window-shop. Or go have apple strudel somewhere because I loved that apple strudel, and read a book. I might call someone and if they weren't home 'Oh well'. I never made any arrangements. And I found this wandering, this sense of reclaiming my life, happened for me on those Saturdays. It was the silence I needed, I needed not to communicate."

MYTH #8
GOOD GENES = HAPPINESS

Are you doomed to your current level of happiness due to your genes? Does each person have a set point that cannot be varied?

Research on twins suggests that genetics can account for up to 50 percent of their level of well-being. A person's circumstances, such as their cultural region, demographics, personal experience, and life status, might account for up to 10 percent.[18] This leaves us with at least 40 percent of our happiness that is entirely determined by how we intentionally choose to respond to our life circumstances. Adopting the strategies in the next section is what you *can* do and what *can* make a difference in your life.

Take charge of your 40 percent and you will surely see the results. Let me show you how . . .

SECTION 4

22 Happiness Strategies

So, if income, life circumstance, gender, and attractiveness are not likely to make a significant difference, what's left? If these things do not increase happiness, then what does? This is where we delve into the things that *actually* do make a difference in happiness levels. It's time to fill your cup, and I have strategies for you to do just that. And guess what? They are all free!

When researching this book, I looked for studies on things that could lead us to be happier in our essence, that give us a sense of calm and gratification. They may not seem as exciting as the ones that television makes you think you'll feel when you lose 10 pounds, get a new wardrobe, and get a makeover. But they are deeper, more authentic, and longer lasting. Not as fragile or transient as pleasure—they are more solid. They might actually make your breath and heartbeat slower rather than excitedly faster. And, of course, they can lead to better health.

Being a happier person is within your control, and actually requires no money and little time. Do I feel happy all the time? No. Do have bad days? Yes. In fact I still use and need the strategies I put together in this book, and often need to remind myself to take my own advice. But my life and that of my child would have been much worse had I not incorporated these changes into my life.

It's all about making the best of the situation and trying to improve it. Use these strategies and make the best of your life!

STRATEGY #1

Try a New Explanatory Style

Oprah's words "Turn your wounds into wisdom" resonate so well with the idea of making the best of your life. As we have seen, scientists say that a person's level of happiness is not based on the number of good or bad events they have experienced (unless they are extreme conditions such as oppression in nondemocratic countries). Rather, it is the attitude and outlook on life that affects happiness.

Scientists have found that some people do not get depressed even after experiencing many bad events while others do. Martin Seligman, one of the founders of positive psychology, discovered that pessimists analyze events in a different way than optimists, and they get depressed more often. He called this the "explanatory style." Seligman considers the explanatory style to be the great "modulator of learned helplessness."[1] "An optimistic explanatory style stops helplessness, whereas a pessimistic explanatory style spreads helplessness," he writes in his book *Learned Optimism*.[2]

Even if you have been a pessimistic, negative thinker for many years, it's not too late to change. "One of the most significant findings in psychology in the last twenty years," says Seligman "is that individuals can choose the way they think."[3] Adopting a positive explanatory style will do wonders for you and your children, and you can learn how to do so. It can help you to unlearn previous feelings of helplessness, teach you that what you do is not futile, and perhaps even prevent you from sinking into depression. And we can learn to do it. Seligman writes that "it was clear to us that the remarkable attribute of resilience in the face of defeat need not remain a mystery. It was not an inborn trait; it could be acquired."[4]

People often equate being positive or optimistic with being unrealistic. But in fact, adopting a positive explanatory style does not mean that you ignore reality or become nonobjective. It does not mean that you do not feel sorrow, disappointment, or negative emotions. If something goes wrong or you have a bad experience, being optimistic doesn't mean you have to necessarily see a bad event as something beautiful either. It does not mean chanting happy words or blaming others. That is not realistic. It's more about *not* having destructive thinking when you have setbacks.[5] Having negative emotions is perfectly natural. But the secret to being positive is not to make it bigger than it is!

One of the important differences between happy and unhappy people is how *far reaching* one makes or how much one *magnifies* an incident. Pessimists tend to turn things into catastrophes. This is a fundamental difference between being an optimist and a pessimist.

According to positive psychologists, when a negative event happens, optimists see it as external (not their fault or internal), local (meaning it's specific to one part of life and will not necessarily translate to other areas in their lives), and temporary (having nothing to do with future events). Pessimists personalize the situation; they see it as internal, universal, and permanent.[6]

Optimists have a positive explanatory style for good events as well. If something good happens, they don't brush it off as an isolated incident or as due to some external event. They will explain it as having occurred because of their own efforts, or some other internal attribution. For example, if a pessimist did well on some exam, they might say it was a fluke, or that the teacher must have graded everyone highly. An optimist would explain this as being the result of their studying hard or being smart.[7]

Optimist	Pessimist
I'm having a bad day. The kids are really not cooperating today.	Life really sucks.
I didn't speak nicely to my kid when he spilled the cereal. I'll try to do better next time.	I'm a terrible mother and human being. I always screw up.

Let's take the example of my divorce experience. If I adopt a positive and realistic approach to the fact that my husband left, I would tell myself: "He didn't love me anymore and wasn't attracted to me."

You may think this isn't very positive. But in fact it is positive and realistic! It is realistic because this is exactly what happened. It is optimistic because I did not magnify the situation and project it into affecting my future. A pessimistic person, on the other hand, might have magnified this experience in *scope* and *time* and perhaps say: "I am so unattractive and no one will ever love me." The experience is the same, but the second approach is the kind of approach that leads to depression. It does not isolate the event, and it extrapolates it into the future. It removes all hope from the future and any control I have over it. It makes me *helpless*.

Optimist	Pessimist
He didn't love me anymore.	No one will ever love me.
He wasn't attracted to me.	I am so unattractive.

The optimistic approach isolates the event. It is something that is out of my control, an anomaly. The optimist believes that things can get better. There is hope. This isolated experience didn't mean no one will love me or that no one will ever find me attractive again (and in fact I was right!). Had I taken the pessimist approach, I would have assumed that I was facing a miserable fate in the future.

We have seen that external circumstances have little to do with your state of happiness. What's important is your state of mind. Learning to have a positive explanatory style can go a long way in the right direction. This is why positive thinking is gaining popularity as an antidepression therapy, especially in light of questions about the safety and effectiveness of antidepressant drugs.

In case you needed another little impetus for getting a new attitude, then how about the prevention of osteoporosis? In 2007, research done by Giovanni Cizza, MD, Ph.D., of the National Institute of Mental Health (NIMH) revealed that the blues can eat away at your bones at least as much as inadequate calcium or smoking. According to the findings, women ages 21–45 who are even mildly depressed have thinner bones in their hips and backs.[8]

You can take charge and choose to adopt a new explanatory style. First, you need to become aware of what your current style is. One way of investigating what kind of explanatory style you might have is by taking a look at how your children speak. How do they analyze events? Have they copied your explanatory style? It would not surprise me if they have. And how do your parents speak? Research shows that we often learn explanatory styles from our parents.[9] Next time you say something negative or complain about something, stop yourself and write it down. Can you see this event in any other way?

Is your current explanatory style one that you want to live with the rest of your life? Is it the style you want to pass down to your children? If not, it's a good time to start catching your words now! Teach yourself not to be helpless. Teach yourself to always have hope. Don't give up!

"The human body can survive for about thirty days without food. The human condition can sustain itself for about three days without water, but no human alive can survive for more than thirty seconds without HOPE, because without hope we truly have nothing." says Sean Swarner[10] who was diagnosed with two different and unrelated forms of cancer, given a prognosis of just 14 days to live, and read his last rites. He survived both diseases, to the shock of his doctors, and went on to climb Mount Everest with only partial use of his lungs. He continues to inspire everyone around him.

STRATEGY #2

Shift Your Focus

Even the richest, most famous, most beautifully married, and most "skinny" people in the world have plenty they can complain about. They, like us, are capable of focusing on the negative, whatever it might be. Complaining is a favorite pastime of many people. Remove this habit and some people might not have much left to talk about.

We can undo the habit of complaining by consciously altering our focus. What you focus on is your choice. Do you want to focus on the fact you have a few extra pounds to lose, or on the fact that you are healthy enough to exercise? Do you want to focus on the fact that your child doesn't live in a traditional two-parent home, or the fact that he is now in a peaceful environment? As Helen Keller said, "When one door of happiness closes, another opens; but often we look so long at the closed door that we do not see the one which has been opened for us."[11] There are many books written these days about the power of "attracting" things into your life. I'm not sure there are supernatural forces working in this manner. However, I do think that *focus* plays a good part in making things "happen." If you focus on getting a job, you are more likely to get it because you are open to seeing the opportunities when they come. If you focus on finding friends, you are more likely to see the friendliness and potential in a new acquaintance.

The same occurs when you start to focus on the positive in life. Shifting your focus to the positive aspects of life is a choice that can have an immeasurable effect on your well-being. Focusing on the positive brings the positive aspects of life to the forefront and sends the negative dissipating in the air.

Once you get in the habit of focusing on the positive, you will start catching yourself when you get negative and even find it strange. Try to focus on what you love about being a single mother instead of the challenges of it. And take this attitude beyond single motherhood. Being a single mother is but *one* aspect of life. For lasting effects, make a decision on what to focus on for all events in life.

Keeping your mind focused on the positive takes practice. But negative thinking is a habit that can be changed. You might feel odd or strange doing it at first. But as we do it, we start to feel more and more comfortable with our new role and attitude. If you go through the motions, then, as the theory goes, you will start to feel it then own it.

Whenever you catch yourself thinking a negative thought, challenge yourself to find another thought that could easily fit the situation to counterbalance that negative thought. Ask yourself what the facts are, then try to analyze it from different perspective that is still plausible.

At every moment of every day, I bet there is something we could complain about. Our work, being tired, family issues, money, traffic, car repairs, being taken for granted. At every moment of every day, I know we could also choose to focus on something positive: health, a friend that hasn't let us down, food on the table, being in a democratic country with freedom, etc.

I do not walk around simply focusing on the positive all day nor can I say that I never complain. I do. However I think that being acutely aware of the power of my focus has allowed me to complain much less, and with less drama, and to appreciate more. And you can too.

I challenge you to do away with your negative-focus habit. Experts say it takes 21 days to change a habit, so here's a 21-day experiment on complaining about the weather: no matter how hard it is snowing, slushing, sleeting, raining, hailing, or scorching, do not say anything negative about it for 21 days. Indeed, try to find some beauty in it, whatever it is.

If others say, "Can you believe how hot (or cold) (or humid) (or cloudy) it is?" you answer, "It doesn't affect me" or "It's fine with me any way the weather is." Say it out loud so you can hear yourself say it.

After three weeks, I predict that you will actually change your attitude about the weather. In fact, I predict you will never go back to "bitching" about the weather (or at least not to the same extent), and you will see that it feels much better not to have negativity in the morning based on the weather of the day.

Once you practice having a positive focus, you'll find that it will soon feel natural. And of course, you will feel better too. You might even find it odd, or funny, as I do, how people let their days be ruled by the weather. If you are generally neutral about the weather, then choose something else that you typically view negatively for this exercise. Once you achieve this, try another one. If you're up for a real challenge of choosing what to focus on, then try focusing on your strengths rather than on your weaknesses!

STRATEGY #3

Exercise Your Freedom

With your fear, guilt, and self-esteem on the right path, it's time to start exploring and enjoying one of the great new perks of being a single mother—more freedom! The funny thing about freedom is that we may not even realize how long we've done without it until we get it. And when I am talking about freedom, of course I don't mean the freedom to go out and party. I am talking about a more intrinsic feeling of freedom. There are things that I wanted to do when I was married but didn't. To avoid problems, I'd avoid doing what I wanted to do and felt less control over my life. I have married friends who are going through this feeling at the moment. Real freedom is when you don't have to deal with intimidation, guilt, threats, or put-downs; when your choice is respected even when not fully agreed with.

Part of the pleasure of enjoying your freedom is being able to use and trust your instincts. Trusting your instincts is crucial to having a happy, fulfilling life. Happy people have work that is meaningful *to them*. They have hobbies and goals that are interesting and important *to them*, that involve *their* abilities, rather than work, goals, or hobbies that they are pressured into. To discover these, you need to look inside, know yourself, and trust yourself. In other words, you need to be true to yourself. I have found that it takes incredible courage simply to be yourself. So follow *your* lead, *your* intuition, and do what is interesting and important to *you*! Exercise your freedom! This will inevitably lead to greater happiness!

Feel free to have friends come over. Feel free to cook the food you like. Feel free to wear torn, cozy pajamas. Feel free to join some group or workshop that you always wanted to join. Feel free to pursue the work or projects that *you* like or dreamed of.

I know that for many women it's hard to enjoy freedom after a separation because they have yet to learn what to do with it. Many women will confess that they don't even know what they like or don't know what to do with their time, if they get any. They simply do not know themselves anymore. They have spent so much energy dealing with a difficult relationship or trying to solve problems, that there was no head space for thinking beyond that. If you have been in a certain mind-set for a long time, it's difficult to switch. But you no longer have to spend time thinking about whether he's cheating, whether he loves you, or whether the relationship will work. This might free up some space in your mind for some new thoughts.

It's time to discover yourself. Give yourself time. Slowly discover what you like and love! Get started by thinking about your childhood or anytime before entering your relationships for those who were in one. What kind of music did you like? Put it on in the house. Let your inner voice out by singing out loud no matter what your voice sounds like to others. Ask yourself what kind of sports you used to like? Try them again. What kind of arts did you like? What kind of personality did you have as a child? Try to rediscover yourself and trust your own instincts.

For some of us, the freedom of being single has meant having the freedom to experience new romantic or sexual experiences. And for others, it has meant to get new and better partners, *if this is what you want*. Not all single mothers are hoping to find a new, long-term committed relationship; many say they prefer to stay single or in some other noncommitted arrangement. Our needs are not all the same nor are our circumstances.

As one woman mentioned on a message board online: "Tonight I bought a new set of sheets for my bed, beautiful deep pink with lavender blossoms scattered on them—and after I washed and dried them with my new lavender and vanilla fabric softener, I put them on my bed and rolled around in them—and it hit me. I feel more like an adult who makes my own choices now that I'm single than I ever did as part of a couple."

STRATEGY #4

Be Open to Possibilities

The media often report "scientific" facts about what the "average" or the "majority" of our society is up to. We hear statements like: "Most people think that...," "The majority of people will...," "8 out of 10 women...," "The average American will..." These are generalizations that lead to stereotypes.

But what about those who are *not* in that average? These are the ones who are interesting to know about! If we focus just on what most of the other people are up to, we might think that we have to be part of them. This can limit us. Let's explore the possibilities by deciding that we're not going to be swayed by generalizations.

If, for example, the average person gains two pounds a year, or the majority of new businesses fail, this means that there are people who *do not* gain weight every year, and there are businesses that *do* succeed. Let's focus on those! What did they do right? What can we learn from them? How can we succeed like them, instead of resigning to being one of the majority. Think about this next time we hear someone say "Most single mothers are..."

Does it matter what studies show about the "average" single mother, the average woman, the average North American, or any other average? Let's focus on what the best or exceptional do and not just the average or majority. If they can achieve something, even if there are fewer of them, then this means achievement is *possible*—and if it's possible for them, it's possible for us as well. History is full of people who never settled for being one of the majority: Martin Luther King Jr., Mahatma Gandhi, Mother Teresa, Nelson Mandela, Oprah Winfrey. The list goes on and on.

STRATEGY #5

Find a Role Model

One good way of getting yourself on the path to improving your attitude and life is to have a good role model. Do you know someone who is always complaining about everything and sees only the negative in everything? If so, this is *not* your ideal role model. In fact, I would recommend that you distance yourself for a while from such people so that they don't bring you down while you're trying to develop your new approach to life.

As single mom Sally (not her real name) points out: "I have some divorced friends, but I really try not to get into that thing of bitching about your ex-husband because we could all get down in that gutter so fast."

Find some positive people and hang around them. Learn from their attitude. What do they complain about and what do they not complain about? Learn and practice, learn and practice, learn and practice! Or find another single mother who seems to feel "OK" and "happy" most of the time despite the challenges and low moments, who seems to cope well with her problems.

Try reading about other people's lives. Many people have lived many ups and downs, and reading about how they coped with their experiences can offer inspiration. Your role models don't have to be perfect, nor do you have to admire everything about them. Perhaps there is just one aspect about them that you can relate to and learn from. They can offer insight into coping with concerns you are dealing with at the moment.

For example, I admire people who have the courage to express their thoughts peacefully and authentically, while remaining open to understanding and learning from others. It is a great skill which I am continuing to try to develop. I also admire people like Norma Bastidas, who show amazing displays of overcoming adversity. She is a Canadian single mother who started running at the age of 40 to relieve the stress of dealing with her son's illness. She's now running ultra-marathons around the world to raise money for vision-impaired kids. Those of us who might have tried running know that it's not easy to run for 10 minutes, let alone ultra-marathons up to 250 kilometers, over several days. And the ultra-marathons she's running are in unbelievably difficult places, with extreme weather conditions, elevations, and challenges. She achieved her goal of running seven ultra-marathons in seven continents in seven months and has now started a new challenge: she plans to be the fastest female to climb the highest summit on each continent—and to achieve all these climbs in 12 months. She has overcome poverty, rape, abuse and addiction and is an amazing example of the power of human beings. You can read more about her mission to raise money for charities at www.normabastidas.com.

Many of us don't have to look far for role models. For Lara (not her real name), single mother of two, it's her mother. "I was raised by a single mother. My mother raised four girls on her own. My mother is everything to me. We never missed out on anything. She was always there for us. I knew that if she was able to do it I would find the energy to do it myself also. My mother inspired a lot. She was my role model ... This is a woman who comes from Eastern Europe, who didn't have an education, who had to clean for a living ... who worked very hard, and we all turned out great."

Cheryl chose strong women as role models. "My aunt is a very strong woman. My mom is a very strong woman. ... And my lawyer ... very strong feminist women. And that really helped me." She added that talking to strong women also helped her to let go of old-fashioned notions of what a family is supposed to look like. It made her "proud of this new life ... that I was handling it and I looked forward to it—the independence and the strength that I was gaining from this," she said.

Though not a single mother, Anita Roddick was another unstoppable woman. She passed away in 2007, leaving behind a life full of amazing achievements. She started selling soaps from her garage to make a living for her daughters while her husband was trekking the Americas. Her company grew to more than 2,000 stores, known as the Body Shop, with annual revenue of $680 million. She then sold her company and immersed herself in campaigns on environmental, fair-trade, human-rights, and social-justice issues. And she had an amazingly strong attitude. "A woman in advancing old age is unstoppable by any earthly force," she declares. Her role model: Joan of Arc.[12]

Another person I learn from is the young woman I mentioned earlier from the Philippines. Though her husband and daughter are back home until she will be able to process their immigration papers, which takes years, she is a wonderfully smiley, positive, and noncomplaining person. She's always laughing and calm.

I was also fortunate enough to have parents that are both strong, optimistic, and noncomplainers. Surely their attitudes have rubbed off on me, and I am grateful for their lessons.

I encourage you to find role models who are not only single mothers, or women for that matter. Although your primary role is that of being a single mother, I would shy away from feeling like this it your "label." You may also be: sister, friend, businesswoman, teacher, environmentalist, feminist, or, my favorite "label"—a person.

Most people have valuable information and advice to offer about some area of life. We can learn something from everyone! The key is to identify what each person has to offer and go to that person for that area of expertise. I ask different people for advice when I need help with parenting, business, fitness, and computers. From others, it's more subtle. From someone who talks a lot or disregards others, we may learn to look at ourselves and see if we are doing the same. From someone who listens well, we learn to emulate. Be open to learning from everyone you encounter, and your growth and transformation is inevitable.

STRATEGY #6

Do Not Keep Up with the Neighbors

Are you obsessed with the accumulation of material goods? As we have seen, in developed countries, once the basic needs of food and shelter and safety are met, having extra income will not lead to a significant increase in happiness.

All the material goods in the world can still leave people feeling empty. Some of the richest people in the world are miserable. When was the last time spending money actually made you a happier person? It won't.

Interestingly enough, money *can* make you happy if you give it away! University of British Columbia graduate student Lara Aknin and Harvard researcher Michael Norton found that people who gave money to charity or bought gifts for friends found greater happiness. And it didn't matter whether they spent $5 or more, as long as it was for others.[13]

It is clear that we should not be focusing our efforts on accumulating more and more material goods. Instead of feeling guilty because you can't afford to buy your children more material goods, consciously choose to buy them less. They might actually end up being more grateful for what they have!

Do your children have more than you had when you were a child? How many things do they receive and ignore 10 minutes later? How many miserable children with rich parents have you seen? I suggest it's because we give them too much ... or too much of the wrong things.

If you really want to give something valuable to your child, give your time. Give an experience. Give a lesson. Give a smile or a hug. Give them space to grow. These are things that will stick with them, not an extra toy. Material things cannot make you or your children happy. In fact, I think they can sometimes make things worse!

I have adopted an approach of "less is more" in my home. I try to constantly get rid of things I don't need. I encourage my son to do the same, and we're always dropping things off at charities. Material things will not bring happiness. Having fewer things actually makes me feel better because there is less clutter. Get rid of half your clothes. You'll feel relieved. Throw away all that unnecessary stuff. The less you have, the less there is to clean and organize!

Instead of focusing on the material, focus on work or activities that engage your strengths and skills—and that you enjoy. Try to find something in your life that is meaningful to you or that gives you the kind of challenge you need—try to find what is called the "zone." When we are in this "zone," we feel challenged and get completely absorbed. Psychologist Mihaly Csikszentmihalyi calls this feeling "flow," and it makes people feel satisfied with life.[14] Even if you find a job that pays less, you are probably better off finding work that is interesting and challenging to you and uses your skills, than one that doesn't meet those criteria. And it doesn't have to be "professional" work. I know a receptionist at a dentist office who seems to be perfectly suited for her work and very satisfied. She is very sociable and therefore interacts with patients in the waiting room all day offering them conversation and cheerfulness. Flow can be experienced in leisure as well. Watching a big-screen TV cannot make you feel very great because it doesn't engage your skills. To get into a state of flow, you would need to find an activity that uses your skills, such as painting, socializing, playing an instrument, woodworking, or running.

While in a state of flow, we forget time. We feel immersed. We forget our worries. Letting go of the ideas surrounding material gain will free your mind to explore other activities that can be true sources of happiness.

Imagine if our country's policies were not focused simply on material gains? In the remote Himalayan kingdom of Bhutan, the government considers happiness when making policies. Instead of considering only the gross domestic product (GDP) of the country, it's the only country in the world where the government considers the impact of government policy on the GNH: "Gross National Happiness."[15] When a journalist criticized the slow development of Bhutan in 1987, the king was quoted as saying that "Gross National Happiness is more important than Gross National Product."[16]

The importance placed on the happiness of its people has allowed Bhutan to take radically different approaches than countries that simply focus on wealth. A report from the BBC in 2006 outlines some of Bhutan's decisions, including those banning billboards promoting Coke and Pepsi and other advertising, banning a number of channels including international wrestling and MTV, banning plastic bags, and similar decisions, all made in the name of happiness.[17]

Though I am sure that there are problems to be found in this society, I think we can learn a lot from this little country. "We have to think of human well-being in broader terms," said Lyonpo Jigmi Thinley, Bhutan's home minister and ex-prime minister. "Material well-being is only one component. That doesn't ensure that you're at peace with your environment and in harmony with each other."[18]

Get rid of the unnecessary guilt about what you are able to provide in the material sense to your kids. Money will not necessarily bring you or them more happiness. Instead, focus on spending some time together. Give them a hug in the morning. Talk to them whenever you have time. Cook together. Tell them *and show them* that you love them.

You give but little when you give of your possessions.
It is when you give of yourself that you truly give.

—Kahlil Gibran[19]

STRATEGY #7

Accept Yourself

Today is the perfect day for me to write this section. I had a miserable morning. I lost my patience, yelled at my son, and said words I wish I hadn't. Then I cried and felt terrible. I asked myself, "Who am I to write this book?" After some reflection, I realized that I am nobody and everybody. This is precisely why I should write this book. I am just like all of you. I am learning one day at a time. I have made and will continue to make mistakes. And I know that I have so much more to learn. In other words, I am not an expert, but a student of all the subjects that I have written about in this book. In this regard, we are the same.

I have many days when I doubt myself, when I'm frustrated, and live through the regular ups and downs of life. I've had, and continue to have, very difficult or sad days when I feel like simply crying and giving up. But the skill that I've acquired is to be able to pick myself back up. I try not to beat myself up about things for too long. I apologize when I need to and try to learn from my mistakes. I accept that I am not, and will never be, a perfect parent or person.

This is not an excuse to do wrong. In fact, this is precisely what I was trying to teach my son this morning. The fact that we feel upset during a given moment does not excuse unfriendly behavior. The fact that we understand our imperfect nature does not mean we should not strive to improve. Nor should this understanding be an excuse to rid ourselves from feeling bad about what we may do. On the contrary, it is important to acknowledge where we went wrong, understand it, and try to move forward, toward progress and growth.

But before we can move forward, we must accept today and now. Acceptance means acknowledging and not fighting the truth of today. It means accepting this point and the point you are at today.

It's easy to see the source of our bad days. Many of us have had to deal with childhood traumas. Many of us have had adult trauma related to our divorce or other events. Some of us don't have much support from family or friends. And most of us have so much responsibility it's hard to even take the time to reflect on life or on how to improve it. With all this, why expect ourselves to be perfect adults or parents? We are human. We are doing our best. We are trying to make the best life for ourselves and our children. We *will* make mistakes. We don't need to beat ourselves up about those days when things really don't go well. In order to move forward, we need to accept where we are right now.

I don't think we should ever focus on "fixing ourselves," "changing," or "becoming" someone or something else. It is more about *growing*. And self-acceptance is a crucial stepping-stone to growth. Accept yourself, who you are, what you've done, and what you've been through. Stop fighting this moment you are in. It is only once you have done that, that you are in a position to grow. So acceptance is not resignation. It is a stepping-stone to growth.

The strategies in this book are aimed at helping you see things that might improve life but won't make it anywhere near "perfect." They can show you where you have power to make things better than they are right now, and this is what it's all about. Improvement—knowing that we can improve your home, your relationship with your children, and their outlook for the future, one day at a time, the best way we can, whatever that might be on that particular day. Just don't give up!

The next time there is chaos in your home or in your head, accept it. It's part of life, part of being human. Try to learn something from that experience. Try to fix what broke as much as possible and move forward. Women, and especially mothers, do so much good for the world. Their goodness always outweighs the days where things are all wrong.

I accept where I am today. I also apologized to my son and took responsibility for this morning. I hope from this morning that he has learned not to make excuses for wrong behavior, to take responsibility for wrong actions, to apologize when it's necessary. And to forgive and move forward. I have learned these things as well.

STRATEGY #8

Be Grateful

The hardest thing to see is what is in front of your eyes.

—Johann Wolfgang von Goethe[20]

There's an old Yiddish story about a poor man who lived with his wife, six children, and his mother in a very small, one-room house. He was miserable with all the noise and chaos in his small house. "Go see the rabbi," his wife suggested. After telling the rabbi his problem, the rabbi said, "When you get home, take your chickens and bring them into your house to live with you." The man did as he was told. After a week of enduring the chickens in the house, he ran back to the rabbi for help. "What have you done to me, Rabbi?" he cried. "It's awful. I did what you told me and the chickens are all over the house!" The rabbi said calmly, "Do you have a goat? Go home and put your goat to live with you in the house." The man couldn't understand why the rabbi would do this but listened to him. After another week, he could bear it no more and ran back to the rabbi. "The goat is smashing up all the furniture; the chickens are causing a terrible mess! Please help me!" he moaned. The rabbi said, "Go home now and bring your cow to live with you in the house." He was anguished but did what he was told. After several more days, he ran back to see the rabbi in desperation. "I can't live like this." He cried, "It's like living in a stable, with the cow, the goat smashing the furniture, and the chickens eating everything in sight. Please help me!" In a sweet voice, the rabbi answered, "Now go and take all the animals out of your house." The man ran back to his house and took all the animals out of the house. His family slept well for the first time in weeks, and he was relieved.

He ran back to the rabbi the next morning and said, "We have such a good life, the animals are out of the house, and everyone is joyful!"

Being grateful is the opposite of taking things for granted, and it's essential for happier living. In every moment, there are aspects of life that are difficult and others that are good. It's really a question of what we choose to focus on. Being grateful for the good helps us feel that life is good instead of awful.

We have all heard that having a grateful outlook can lead to greater peace of mind, happiness, and physical health. This sounds compelling, but has it been scientifically tested? In fact, there's plenty of research on the effects of gratitude on one's psychological and physical well-being.

Psychologist Sonja Lyubomirsky studies factors that affect levels of happiness. In one study, she focused on the effects of having a gratitude journal. The results of her research revealed that subjects who wrote in their gratitude journal once a week for six weeks experienced a clear increase in their overall satisfaction with life compared to the control group.[21]

Psychologist Robert Emmons, from the University of California at Davis and author of *Thanks!: How the New Science of Gratitude Can Make You Happier*, has been studying gratitude for more than 10 years, and found that gratitude exercises can improve physical health, raise energy levels, and even relieve pain and fatigue in patients with diseases. The practice of gratitude, such as writing in gratitude journals, can increase happiness levels by up to 25 percent.[22] "The ones who benefited most tended to elaborate more and have a wider span of things they're grateful for," he notes.[23]

Basically, we can help our hypertension and overall health, be better able to cope with stress, sleep better, become more optimistic about life, and have vitality just by learning to be more grateful. And being grateful has been shown to improve connectedness with others, to encourage reciprocity and friendships, which can lead to an improved support system.[24]

We are often so busy thinking of the future, we forget to be grateful for our present. "I have to pick up my son from school, drop off this, pick up this, do this, do that." When this happens too much, our minds are in the future never enjoying the present. Living in the present means enjoying and being grateful for your present moment. It means not always trying to get more and more and more. Just enjoy the smile from your child, a long bath, a hug from a friend, reading one page of a book before falling asleep at night.

Some of you might think that it is difficult to be grateful when you feel you have many problems. But we all have troubles, and many people in the world are, of course, much worse off than we are. Try not to compare yourself to people who seem to have a "perfect life." Everyone has different troubles and we don't always know what's going on in other people's lives. To enjoy life, we need to make the best of our situation and find the beauty in whatever it is offering us.

I am sure that you can find some little aspects of your day that you are grateful for. How about: I am grateful for the delicious ice cream I shared with my son today. I am grateful for being able to sleep in a warm bed in peace. I am grateful for my health and that of my child. I am grateful for my neighbor. I am grateful for the clean, hot water that comes out of my tap in abundance! Do you know how many people in the world would only *dream* to have the list I just mentioned?

I asked my son, at age eight, what he thinks of being grateful. He said, "It's good to be grateful because if you always want and want and want, then you never have a smile and you're never happy." Of course I have been speaking to him about this for years, but I think he's starting to get it.

Try starting a Gratitude Journal with your kids. Get them to tell you, every evening, three things they are grateful for and write it down. I cannot imagine a better souvenir to give your children when they are older than a journal about the good stuff.

Make gratefulness a way of life. Happiness, said Benjamin Franklin, "is produced not so much by great pieces of good fortune that seldom happen as by the little advantages that occur every day."[25]

STRATEGY #9

Simplify

Women still do the majority of the housework, despite any gains in women's rights and regardless of whether they work outside the home. Interestingly enough however, studies like those conducted by labor economist Helene Couprie of Toulouse University show that single women do less housework than women in a couple! Men, on the other hand, actually do less housework on average once they begin living as a couple. In other words, even when a man's housework is taken into account, he causes additional labor for his spouse.[26] So for many mothers who are married, especially those living as single mothers while being married (*de facto* single mothers), it is even more difficult than being on your own in this regard. Of course, there are always men who participate a great deal, so I do not want to discredit those. But unfortunately, statistics show this is not the usual case.

Whatever your housework load is, managing time is a necessity for a single mother. I found that one of the best strategies to save time is to adopt a simpler life materially speaking. Fewer things means fewer things to clean, organize, keep track of, insure, repair, etc. Material things take up your time whether you realize it or not. The time they rob from you is sometimes subtle, but look closely and you will soon see that this is true. If the closet is cluttered, then it takes up *time* by making you have to search longer to find things. If a shelf is full and something falls and breaks, then it takes *time* to clean it up. Having a lot of things requires your time and attention in one way or another.

Limit the number of things you have that can steal your time. Then find strategies to decrease your current workload. For example, buy only one or two colors of socks for each person of the family.

This makes sorting socks a simple task. Place cutlery in a drawer without the plastic separator. Saves time on sorting unnecessarily. Try to find a job close to schools and home. And pay less attention, spend less time, and spend less money on how you look. Focus more on having a healthy body and mind and your beauty will shine though whatever outfit you wear.

Simplify your daily routines as well. Why do so many parents feel compelled to register their kids in so many activities? One or maybe two activities a week seems like more than enough to me. In fact, some researchers question the benefits of any such activities. Activities often focus on improving skills, whether it's dance, soccer, baseball, or tennis. This might be OK, but what happened to letting children simply play for fun without the pressure of improvement? We will discuss "empty time" for children further in the next section.

Not racing around to activities frees up more time for everyone and allows for some home time and downtime. Think about your own childhood. Are your best memories attached to family time, or going to gymnastics classes?

It takes courage to choose simplicity, and to ignore what everyone else is buying and doing. Start choosing for yourself what is important to you and your family. Making your life simpler will enable you to focus on what is more meaningful in life. And this is definitely more valuable in the long run than "stuff."

STRATEGY #10

Limit Your Choices

American psychologist Barry Schwartz and author of *The Paradox of Choice: Why More Is Less* says that most of us assume that having more choices will make us happier.[27]

But Schwartz thinks we might have too much of a good thing and has changed my perception of choices permanently. To make his point about the paradox of choice, he counted the number of salad dressings in his supermarket and found that there were 175 varieties, not including the varieties of olive oil and balsamic vinegars. There were also 285 varieties of cookies and 230 kinds of soup.

Similarly, he notes the explosion of choices in so many aspects of life, not only what we purchase in stores. He does not discount the benefits of choice compared to the limited choices of previous generations, but what Schwartz points out is that there might also be a negative effect from the complexity and excessiveness of choices.

The first negative effect, he notes, is that having too many choices sometimes makes us feel paralyzed instead of liberated. We often have to put so much time and effort into making decisions, even trivial ones, that we often just don't know what to do. "It causes you to worry, if you choose without having explored all the possibilities, that maybe you've made a mistake."[28]

I think Schwartz is tapping into an experience we can all relate to but perhaps have not been consciously aware of. How many times have I passed by a shop where bras are sold and decided to pass right by because there were too many to choose from that it felt overwhelming? How many of us find it overwhelming to choose summer camps when there are so many choices? I find it so hard to choose a shampoo when there are hundreds on the shelf, each promising such wonderful results. This is something we go through on a constant basis in so many areas of our lives.

The second negative effect Schwartz notes is that, even when we make decisions, we often end up less satisfied than if we had fewer choices. If, for example, we buy a shampoo, we always think that maybe another one would have been better. We even blame ourselves for making such bad decisions. The missed opportunity, he says, diminishes satisfaction.[29] Indeed.

I have been trying to be aware of the negative effects of too many choices, especially regarding choices that are of no major consequence. And, since I like to follow ideas with action, I have also taken steps to reduce my stress related to excessive choice and even changed the way I present choices to my son.

The next time I went looking for a shampoo, I refused to be part of the excessiveness of choice and quickly gave myself three choices from brands I already knew. I told myself that these are all "good enough." I then chose one, and I went home relaxed and satisfied.

When I went to buy running shoes for my son, instead of checking five stores and comparing many shoes, I went into one store, compared three that seemed fine, and chose one. I told myself that the three were good enough. I didn't put the pressure on myself to try to find "the best quality for the best value"—it's a never-ending process! I try to remove any "regret" thoughts of the kind that there might be a better purchase elsewhere, and I left the store feeling relaxed and satisfied.

When traveling, I now refuse to overanalyze the 100 hotels to choose from. I choose one that seems to makes sense and is OK. It's usually just fine, good enough, and does not affect my life in any way. I save myself a lot of stress and time, and manage to be satisfied with what I have.

So what if the hairdresser isn't perfect, the shampoo isn't the best, and the kids could have gone to a "better" camp. So what if I could've had a slightly "better" hotel.

I later realized that there is a word that is used by researchers for this approach. It is called to "satisfice," namely, "to be satisfied with an option that is merely 'good enough,' without concern for alternative, potentially better options."[30] And guess what? Happy people tend to satisfice!

Unhappy people, on the other hand, usually try to maximize and make the absolutely best possible choice ("maximizers"), whether it be about a stroller, a job, or a school. "For people like this, choice overload can be a nightmare, for the only way to know you've got the best is by examining all the alternatives, by doing an exhaustive, and exhausting, search. And the impossibility of doing such a search almost guarantees that you'll regret decisions, even if they're good," says Schwartz.[31] And although their decisions may ultimately lead to an objectively better result (e.g., best stroller at best price) *maximizers* are not as happy as *satisficers*.[32] The simple lesson, says Schwartz, is not to be a maximizer![33]

Let go of having to make perfect decisions on things, at least regarding noncritical issues. You might find, as I have, that it is very liberating. You can do the same when presenting choices to your children. It removes a lot of analysis and stress that might not be even leading to better lives. There is amazing freedom in making life simpler.

STRATEGY #11

Take Care of Yourself

We all try to give as much as we can to our children. As single mothers we are tempted to overcompensate for what we think our children might be missing due to living with a single parent. Ironically, however, when we give too much of ourselves, or ignore our needs, we might end up giving *less*.

You might ask how taking care of yourself is possible when there is so little time. Why waste time on yourself when there are so many more important things to do? The reasons are simple. First, because you deserve it. So what if you have to say no to someone so that you can take a bath, read a book, or simply take 15 minutes to do nothing? Your bath is important! Doing nothing is important!

Second, if you feel better, you will be better able to use your time wisely, be able to make better decisions, see life more clearly and make better plans—all of which are good for everyone in the household. If taking a bath leads to you decide to stop interacting with a negative friend, for example, you've done yourself and your family a service. You probably gained more well-being, energy, and vitality for other tasks.

Most importantly, single mothers must take care of themselves because if they don't, and get ill or are less capable of coping as a result, their children will suffer. If a single mother burns out, it's critical, more so than in a two-parent household, for obvious reasons. There is often no one to take over the responsibilities and the children when we are down. They really need you to be healthy and balanced!

Don't let your children's reactions stop you from doing what you know you should do regarding yourself or your household. It makes sense to consider and weigh the children's feelings when making a decision, but this is not the same as being afraid of their reactions. Your kids may object or not understand the importance of certain things, including your happiness and well-being. That's OK. They will perhaps understand as adults. Or, maybe they won't, but it still doesn't matter. I think it's our duty as mothers, and especially as single mothers, to take care of our own well-being. This isn't selfish; it's extremely necessary *and* it's your responsibility. If you are not well, you will be unable to take care of your children properly. If you want to give them a happy and functional mother, it's crucial for you to take care of yourself. It is better to give 85 percent of yourself in balanced manner than to give 100 percent and lose it!

So the next time you find yourself with a few minutes near a shop, don't spend it looking for more kids' clothes. They probably have enough to manage. Buy something you need! The next time you have a few moments to spare before you go to sleep, don't prepare a perfect lunch for the lunchbox. Take a shower or read a favorite book! Instead of thinking what kids' activities you're going to do, choose something you like to do and drag them along. And do so without any guilt! In fact, I refuse to constantly go to wild kiddy places that make me crazy with overstimulus. This is not to say you should never do kids' activities—amusement parks or the like—but rather to limit them and ensure they are balanced with what *you* like and need. Your kids will appreciate them more as well. And you might be happier hanging out with them. I'd much prefer going for a walk while my son bounces a basketball. This way he gets a happier mother—and that's a good thing for me (and for him).

The happier you are, the happier your children will be. Take care of yourself for the sake of your children. Take some time for yourself, free your mind and don't feel guilty about it, even if it means focusing less on your kids' needs (or wants). They will have a better parent and therefore a better life. And so will you and you deserve it!

STRATEGY #12

Sleep Well

When we sleep well, or neglect to, it affects our health, happiness, and overall well-being. One of the simplest things you can do to get more sleep is not waste time watching too much TV or other useless activities instead of sleeping. Spending time thinking in bed can also affect your ability to sleep. Our brains are often at full speed even as we lay our head on the pillow. We think about what we need to do the next morning, or what we need to remember, or what we should check, or who we need to call. One simple solution to cut out some of these thoughts is to keep your agenda or papers on your nightstand. When you have a thought, write it down so you don't have to worry about forgetting it. Tell yourself you will deal with it tomorrow.

I also recommend you have some kind of positive or calming book handy that you can read before going to sleep. You might read for only three minutes before falling asleep (which is what typically happens to me) but you still end up dozing off in a positive place.

If you are not convinced of the importance of sleep, here is some science: According to David Niven's research in *100 Simple Secrets of Happy People*, "Quality and quantity of sleep contribute to health, well being, and a positive outlook. For those who sleep less than 8 hours, every hour of sleep sacrificed results in an 8% less positive feeling about the day."[34] This applies to your kids as well.

Robert Stickgold, a cognitive neuroscientist at Harvard Medical School and Beth Israel Deaconess Medical Center in Boston who studied the effect of sleep on learning and memory, said that "sleep is the glue that binds new information into the brain." In one of his studies, he taught volunteers how to perform a task, then measured how quickly they completed it. The results showed that people tested later the same day they were taught showed no improvement. Those allowed to sleep for at least six hours after being taught improved 15 percent.[35]

If you are having trouble falling asleep, try some sleep strategies suggested by experts on the Internet. (Some of the tips on the Internet won't apply to us, such as "avoid napping during the day.") Common tips are to avoid caffeine at certain times of the day, relax before bedtime, don't go to bed too hungry or too full, get regular exercise, and of course, avoid stressful TV shows before bed. Watching TV before going to bed can contribute to poor sleep or insomnia. After you fall asleep, your brain continues to process the drama which leads to interrupted sleep patterns even after the TV is off.

If you need another good reason to put sleep as a priority, how about losing weight? Researchers at Stanford University School of Medicine found that sleep loss leads to higher levels of a hormone that triggers appetite and lower levels of a hormone that tells your body it's full—leading to weight gain.[36] "It's a technology issue," says Dr. Helen Driver, an adjunct professor of medicine at Queen's University and president of the Canadian Sleep Society. "People have computers and TVs in their bedrooms, they eat or read e-mail before they go to bed. The result is they don't get a restful sleep. But I would say that if you're sleep-deprived and you follow good sleep hygiene, you will lose weight without changing much else."[37]

If you have troubles keeping you up at night, then these need to be addressed. I know that my mind chatter is the worst at night. I can spend a lot of time reliving past experiences, reviewing decisions, making plans, and going crazy when I should be sleeping. To combat the invasion of these unwanted thoughts, I try to meditate in bed, repeating one word over and over, or focusing on my breath until my brain turns off. But mostly, I try to keep my mind, body, and anxiety levels as healthy as possible using the strategies I have learned from writing this book so that I am more capable of handling difficult situations when they arise. I always remind myself of this famous quote by an unknown author: "The most effective sleeping pill—peace of mind."

STRATEGY #13

Listen to Music

Most of us enjoy listening to music, but here's the science behind it. Numerous studies have found that our mood is affected positively if we listen to music we like. And some studies show that students who listen to certain music while writing exams or doing tasks perform better overall on such tasks. So music is good not only for infants, but for all of us at all ages.

Angela Clow, a professor of psychophysiology at Westminster University in England and a world authority on the biochemistry of stress, found that pleasant music can boost the immune system (as does the smell of chocolate!). She also compared patients in a day-surgery waiting room that had music playing and art on the walls against ones without music or art. She found that the art and music patients had lower heart rates, blood pressure, and cortisol, and needed less sedation before their surgery.[38]

According to a Finnish study published in 2008, music helps people recover more quickly from strokes. The study involved 60 people who recently had a stroke. One group listened to their favorite music every day, one to audio books, while the third group didn't listen to any music. Those who listened to music showed a 60 percent improvement in verbal memory after three months compared to 17 percent for those who listened to audio books and 29 percent for those who listened to neither.[39]

I met a single mother once who clearly understood the importance of music. She recounted the story of her divorce and moving into a new apartment with her children. Wanting to start a new life, she had decided to leave all the furniture, even if it meant that she would be able to furnish her new place only slowly, paycheck by paycheck. On the first night in the new apartment, she remembers how strong the echo was as she walked on the floors because there was nothing in the apartment except some blankets and pillows on which she and her kids slept that night. The next day, she grabbed her kids and said they needed to go to the store because "Mommy needed some music." And off they went to get their first music system for the home, before anything else!

Fast forward one year. She got a good job. Her kids are fine. And her house got furnished one piece at a time. After hearing her story, I can see that the pride of having achieved what she did, on her own, was shining through and that music helped start her on that journey.

STRATEGY #14
Turn off the TV

Ask yourself what watching TV has actually brought in your life? People often claim that there are many educational shows, but is this really what you are watching? Tim Kasser, author of *The High Price of Materialism*, discusses how television can negatively impact our lives and self-esteem. He encourages us to exercise our free will. "We can remove activities from our lives that are low flow or that reinforce materialistic values and decrease self-esteem. Put the television in the closet. Cancel your subscription to the glamour and gossip magazines. Stop wandering the mall or shopping on the internet. Try to take these activities out of your life and see what happens."[40]

At the very least, try not to watch or read sensationalist news sources or participate in online ranting. Even responsible media outlets can play up dramatic stories that have the effect of frightening the public. If you want to stay informed, pick one or two thoughtful news sources, check in with them long enough to stay informed, then put the newspaper down or turn off the television and computer. If you use TV to wind down, try instead to go to bed with a good book (preferably a calming topic). You will be more rejuvenated the next day than if you had watched a frightening or stressful show right before going to bed. Ideally, keep your TV out of the bedroom altogether.

I actually took the plunge years ago. We have no TV service in our home and it's a huge relief! I cannot flip channels or end up glued to a show for hours that I don't even like. I also don't wake up watching sensationalized news stories. We get our media and news through renting movies, and reading the news in the paper and online. We also occasionally look up whatever topic we might be interested in that day—whether it's practical jokes, Olympics, talks, musicians, etc.—on YouTube.

I often get asked, "Did you hear about the murder of so and so on the news?" Usually, I have not. People want to share terrible details with me, which I am not interested in. I'd rather simply read a headline in the paper or online and decide whether I want to delve into the details about something rather than having the content imposed on me on TV. Do I need to know the gruesome details of every murder? Not really. There is so much other news that has occurred, including positive events that I can read about. TV skews our perception of reality. If you watch too much TV, you will inevitably come to the conclusion that everyone is either very beautiful and rich or about to die a horrible and tragic death. But the best part of turning off the TV is not exposing myself to the constant bombardment of commercials, which we can all do without.

To improve your life, I suggest trying not to watch any TV for one full week. I doubt you will miss it, and you might discover that you will have more time to do useful and interesting things. And get more sleep!

STRATEGY #15

Laugh

Do you believe you can heal yourself of a serious disease by laughing? When prominent political journalist, professor, author, and world peace advocate Norman Cousins returned from Moscow in 1964, he experienced severe joint pain with fever and was diagnosed with *ankylosing spondylitis*, an illness that attacks the connective tissues of the body. He was given a 1 in 500 chance of surviving and he decided to be that 1 in 500.

Cousins's hypothesis was that if negative emotions, such as stress, were bad for your health, then positive emotions could improve health. And since he thought a hospital "was no place for sick people," he checked out of the hospital and into a hotel.

Wanting to get off painkillers, he developed his own recovery program using Vitamin C, a positive attitude, and laughter. He hired a nurse to read funny stories to him. He watched Marx Brothers movies, Candid Camera episodes, and other funny programs. He asked his friends to share any funny stories or jokes they had. He tried to have a hearty laugh several times a day. He found that this laughter was relieving his pain and allowing him to sleep.[41]

Soon he was off of all painkillers and sleeping pills, and despite the prognosis that the connective tissue in his spine was rapidly disintegrating, after several months, he walked out of the hotel recovered and having regained the full function of his body.[42]

He claims that he "laughed himself out of" a deadly disease, and since then, scientists have studied the curative effects of laughter and how it can strengthen your immune system. He eventually returned to work and landed a job as an adjunct professor at the School of Medicine at the University of California.

When Cousins had a heart attack 15 years later, he was convinced that he would recover again. As he was being wheeled into the hospital, he sat up and said, "Gentlemen, I want you to know that you're looking at the darndest healing machine that's ever been wheeled into this hospital." Again, Cousins recovered. He died on November 30, 1990, 16 years after his collagen illness, and 26 years after his doctors diagnosed his heart disease, far surpassing his doctors' predictions. His book, *Anatomy of an Illness as Perceived by the Patient*, describes his "laughing cure" and experiences.

In 1995, in Bombay, young gastroenterologist Dr. Madan Kataria read about Cousins and decided to do something silly. He gathered a few people to meet at a park at 7:00 a.m. to create a laughter club to tell each other jokes and try to make each other laugh. But after a few days, Kataria said, the whole thing became a bit of a flop because people ran out of jokes so started telling sexist jokes or other offending humor. Thinking that the problem might be focusing too much on the reasons for laughing, he gathered this now miserable group again and told them the idea would be to laugh for no reason. Now people started bursting out laughing. Laughter is contagious and soon everyone was participating. Laughter yoga, as it is now called, has been a huge success since. Tens of thousands of people have since joined the laughter movement, claiming health benefits, weight loss, mood elevation, and even treatment of serious disease.[43] Indeed, studies have shown that laughing at a funny film can cause a drop in the stress hormone cortisol.[44]

Believe it or not, a jolly mood can even affect a mother's breast milk! In a 2007 study researcher Hajime Kimata of Moriguchi-Keijinkai Hospital in Japan measured the level of melatonin hormone in the breast milk of nursing mothers before and after they watched a comedy or an ordinary weather report. "Melatonin regulates the sleep-wake cycle and is often disturbed in the allergic skin condition atopic eczema, which all of the 48 babies in the study had. Kimata found that laughing at the funny film, but not hearing the weather report, increased the amount of melatonin in the mothers' milk. In addition, the laughter-fortified breast milk reduced the allergic responses to latex and house dust mites in the infants. Thus, making a nursing mom laugh might sometimes serve as an allergy remedy for her baby."[45]

Laughter strengthens resilience and can help us to see the silver lining when difficult situations arise. And as a side benefit, being more cheerful can help cultivate friendships—which we can all use.

So how can you benefit from this wonder drug? Look for funny movies or situations. Try finding the humor in little things. Put up a funny quote on your wall. I remember taking my son for a haircut at the age of nine. He started laughing uncontrollably every time the hairdresser was trying to use the electric shaver on his neck. His laugh made me laugh, which made the hairdresser laugh which made the client waiting laugh for a long time.

Now it's your turn. Look into a way to laugh more in life. Rent funny movies. Watch a funny show. Go to stand-up comedy. Maybe join a laughter yoga class, a laughter club, or simply get in the habit of laughing more about the ridiculousness of everyday life. My son is an expert at laughing about the funny predicaments he gets into at school. Children are amazing teachers.

STRATEGY #16

Exercise

We all know the benefits of exercise for health, stress, and overall well-being. Countless research has shown that people who exercise feel better about themselves and enjoy life more. I will not preach something that we all already know. What we should explore are the excuses for not doing it. I challenge you to think of one good reason you shouldn't or don't exercise. I imagine the most common excuse is lack of time and energy, and I can certainly relate.

But exercise *must* be built into our lives as a top priority. The effects of lack of exercise are far-reaching into your life and that of your children. The purpose is not necessarily to lose weight, tighten the abs, or get into a miniskirt. The purpose is to increase your physical and mental ability to function well as a parent and human.

I am convinced that exercise is the first "medication" we all need to keep us balanced. Without exercise, I am sure that my mental stability would be greatly affected, especially in times of high stress and tension that seem to constantly creep up in life.

James Blumenthal, Ph.D., professor of medical psychology at Duke University, decided to be one of the first to actually test the effect of exercise in people diagnosed with depression. He asked his patients, who were sedentary men and women over 50, to work out for 30 minutes three times a week. He then compared their response to similarly depressed patients who were on Zoloft or drug and exercise combined. All the patients experienced equally significant reduction in depression symptoms, and had similar remission rates—60 percent to 65 percent.[46]

This means that exercise worked as well as medication! The only difference between the two groups was the initial time it took before there was improvement. It took the exercisers a few weeks longer to start improving than the medication group, but the effects of exercise were longer lasting. "Six months after treatment ended, fewer patients in the exercise group had relapsed into depression."[47]

In other words, exercise not only helps battle depression, but is also preventive medicine in that it can prevent depression from occurring in the first place or its recurrence.

There are ways to find time to exercise. For example, you could exercise at the same time as your kids' activities. I am lucky enough to have found a gym where my son can take karate lessons while I exercise. But even if you both can't do "formal" exercise at the same place, you can still exercise with the kids during their activities. This means either doing exercise with them or doing exercise while they are engaged in their activity. I'm sure your kids have some activity once a week during which you can exercise. For example, when my son was younger and I took him to the park, I would just walk circling the sandbox area while he was playing (instead of sitting on the bench). While he played soccer, I'd circle the field. That's 45 minutes! I might look silly, but I don't care.

If you have lunch at work, then you can use part of it to walk. Or buy a DVD. Maybe you can exercise in your living room. You might even get your kids into it. Even 15 minutes will do wonders. If you like to dance, just put on some loud music and dance around the house for 15–20 minutes. And you can always add walks in funny places. I highly recommend buying an MP3 player so you can have music in your ears to walk in odd places. I have walked back and forth while at airports waiting for flights, in hallways at doctor's offices, and even up and down my three steps outside my home while my son is sleeping in the house. You might think I'm some exercise buff in full shape but I'm not! I have an average body, not slim and with plenty of cellulite and other normal stuff. I do it for my sanity!

You are certainly better off neglecting your children a bit in order to exercise. Instead of giving them 100 percent of what you have (in a miserable and drained way) give 85 percent of a more stable, reasonable, calm, and well-balanced self. I asked my son to tell me about exercise. He said, "One thing my mom thinks a lot, and I think too, is that if you feel sad, then if you exercise you feel happier." My positive brainwashing is working!

STRATEGY #17

Meditate

Most people are no longer used to silence. Everywhere we go we are bombarded with noise, with flat-screen TV's making noise even while we wait for our luggage at the airport, or stand in an elevator. Given the typical loudness of life, it is no wonder that the brain and body need silence. Giving the mind some time for internal stillness is necessary for our physical and psychological health. And meditation is one way to achieve this.

Meditation is so powerful that it has been found to be better than drugs or counseling for depression according to a recent study published in 2008 in the *Journal of Consulting and Clinical Psychology*. The study taught the patients simple techniques of meditation, which they had to practice for 30 minutes a day. After four months, three-quarters of the patients felt so much better they stopped taking medication. Forty-seven percent of patients with long-term depression suffered a relapse, but the figure was 60 percent for those on medication.[48]

Meditation can also have physical effects. In another study on patients with psoriasis, 37 patients were divided into two groups. One group was told to listen and follow the mindfulness meditation instructions on the audio recording during their ultraviolet treatment. The other group also received the treatment but without listening to the tape. The results showed that meditators' skin cleared up four times faster than those who didn't meditate.[49]

There is a multitude of evidence about the benefits of meditation. Meditation is a great way to start changing your life because it can be practiced anytime, anywhere, and has no cost. Its positive effects have been proven since ancient times. Experiments have shown that meditators show stronger immune responses and higher activation in parts of the brain associated with positive mood, including anger regulation. "The same way we train in sports or learn to play chess, we can train the mind to regulate emotion, stabilize attention and become more aware," says Antoine Lutz, a scientist at the University of Wisconsin at Madison who has studied changes in the brains of Buddhist monks.[50]

Indeed, yoga and meditation are known to decrease anxiety, improve moods, change left to right ration in left frontal cortex significantly, strengthen the immune system, and improve intelligence, creativity, memory, and reaction time to stimuli. Meditation has also been said to calm the part of the brain that acts as a trigger for fear or anger.[51]

Does a loud bang make you blink or startle? This is called the startle response, and there is a correlation between anxiety and how easily we startle. People who meditate tend to diminish the quickness of their startle response. His Holiness the Dalai Lama mentioned in an article in the *New York Times* that Dr. Paul Ekman of the University of California at San Francisco told him that "jarring noises (one as loud as a gunshot) failed to startle the Buddhist monk he was testing." Dr. Ekman also told the Dalai Lama that he had never seen anyone stay so calm in the presence of such a disturbance.[52]

Some people think meditation means sitting for an hour in one spot and closing their eyes to relax. In fact, there are many variations. The key is to be present—in the moment. This means neither focusing on the past nor worrying about the future, just being in the here and now. You can try focusing on your breath, saying a mantra, listening to music, progressive muscle relaxation or doing yoga.

The idea is to know and be conscious of what you're doing while you're doing it. When your mind starts to wander, just watch the thoughts pass by and refocus on your breathing or what you were focusing on.

Meditation teaches you how to be in the moment, to stop worrying about the future or living in the past. It is a method to cultivate mindfulness. Mindfulness means paying attention on purpose, being aware of the moment. It is at the heart of Buddhist meditation. But doing nothing takes practice.

I often catch myself thinking about the next thing instead of fully experiencing the present moment. I was reminded of this by my son and his friend, who was at our house one day. We went to the park and then I made burgers for lunch. As we sat down to start eating, I said, "What are you boys going to do now?" My son's friend answered, "We're going to eat these burgers." My son nodded as well. I think children are amazing meditators!

Try to think of the present. Practice being aware of your surroundings. Try to actually look at the leaves outside while walking instead of always thinking about your next destination or task. Savor the coffee you are drinking. Really listen the music on the radio. Look into your children's eyes and be present. And, if you are trying to deal with anxiety and anger issues discussed in Section 2, try to be present to what you feel and observe your body's reactions and your mind's thoughts in order to make sense of what is happening.

> "As you walk and eat and travel, be where you are. Otherwise you will miss most of your life."
>
> —Buddha

And occasionally, whether through meditation, or otherwise, I highly recommend engaging in some activity that temporarily turns off all mental chatter to give your mind a complete break! From the moment we wake up until we sleep, our minds have millions of thoughts racing. Even strenuous exercise like jogging sometimes doesn't turn it off for me. I think one of the only times it turns off completely is when I listen to music or go to my martial arts class, perhaps because it requires serious focus or attention. For some people, painting can turn off the chatter. For others it might be yoga, reading, or knitting. Whatever it is, discover what allows you to be in the moment, allows you to turn off the mental chatter, and try to do this activity more often. It is a technique that can lead to immeasurable rejuvenation.

Try to take a walk today, even if it's for five minutes, without thinking about the past or the future. Walk around aware of every detail you see and smell, without analysis—just observe whatever you see like a movie. Be aware; try not to walk around like a zombie. Notice the wind moving the leaves, the faces of all the people in their cars, the smell of the restaurant you walk by, and your breathing. You are alive. Today! Try to also enjoy silence and especially the silence of your mind. It can bring unspeakable peace.

As Mother Teresa says, "See how nature—trees, flowers, grass—grows in silence; see the stars, the moon and the sun, how they move in silence . . . we need silence to be able to touch souls."[53]

STRATEGY #18

Back to Nature

In 1984, Harvard professor E. O. Wilson claimed that human beings are innately attracted and bonded with nature—that there is something in us that really needs the occasional immersion in nature. He coined the term "biophilia hypothesis" to describe our positive feelings toward nature. Unlike phobias, which are fears about things in our world, philias are the attractions that we have toward certain things in our natural surroundings.

Since then, many scientists have studied how contact with nature, or the lack thereof, could affect an individual's health. For example, studies have shown that patients recovering from surgery in a room with a view of a natural landscape needed less medication, had shorter stays, and complained less.[54]

Ignoring our innate need for nature may have consequences on our well-being, while taking active steps to immerse ourselves in it might actually boost us.

"Ecotherapy," as it is sometimes called, boosts well-being. A study carried out by Essex University for the charity Mind compared the effects of walking in a park and walking in an indoor shopping center. Seventy-one percent of the participants reported decreased levels of depression after the green walk. Only 45 percent of those in the shopping mall said their depression was improved, 22 percent had an increase in depression, and half said they felt more tense afterwards. Ninety percent had increased self-esteem after the country walk, while 44 percent reported a decrease in their self-esteem after window shopping in the shopping center.[55]

Make an effort to spend some time outdoors. What better way to spend time than with the greatest single mother of all, mother nature! In the words of Anne Frank, "The best remedy for those who are afraid, lonely or unhappy is to go outside, somewhere where they can be quiet, alone with the heavens, nature and G-d. Because only then does one feel that all is as it should be and that G-d wishes to see people happy, amidst the simple beauty of nature. As long as this exists, and it certainly always will, I know that then there will always be comfort for every sorrow, whatever the circumstances may be. And I firmly believe that nature brings solace in all troubles."[56]

STRATEGY #19

Work Toward Your Goals

When I was in university, in my early 20s, I was full of goals and dreams. Somewhere along the way, they faded. When women get married, we often replace our goals with our partner's goals, and work at helping them get there. Becoming a single mother certainly ended that behavior! It was now time to find my own goals.

Studies have shown that one of the best predictors of happiness is whether a person considers his or her life to have a purpose. Without a purpose, it's easy to feel unsettled.

Indeed, having a goal, *even if it's not attained*, still makes people happy. The process of moving toward it, and making progress, is often more important than achieving it! It keeps us feeling alive and excited about life. It gives us a sense of controlling our lives, which also leads to more happiness.

I challenge you to take the time to develop a goal for yourself. Make it something interesting to you, which uses your strengths and values. Your goal should not be based on what people think but rather what *you* think is important according to *your* own interests and values. You have to identify the things you want to do. It's important to trust yourself when choosing these goals. Most of us have some idea of what they are.

Your goal could be to be a better parent, to be a good friend, to make money, to start your own business, to get a degree, to make more friends, to find a partner, to run a marathon—anything!

Although parenting and our children are usually a key element in our lives, and I believe we all have goals relating to our children, I would recommend trying to find some goals that are separate from raising your children. Many parents get their self-esteem exclusively from having good children who achieve in school, or are competent in other ways. Pride in their children and their need to look like good parents is so strong that they end up using their children to bring themselves a feeling of self-worth and self-esteem. I suspect this puts undue pressure on the children to be who their parents want them to be.

Other than having a purpose related to our children, we should find a purpose or goal related to a hobby, charity, or work. "When [a] person enjoys his or her work, whether it is paid or unpaid work, and feels that it is meaningful and important, this contributes to life satisfaction," says Ed Diener. "When work is going poorly because of bad circumstances or a poor fit with the person's strengths, this can lower life satisfaction."[57]

Once you've figured out some goals, write them down and post them in front of you in your home. Then make them happen! Making some general statement of a goal is usually not enough if you actually want to achieve it. You will need to break it down into pieces, *very specific pieces*, and put them into your agenda.

For example, if one of your goals is to be a better parent, it's not enough to just say "My goal is to be a better parent" and post that up on your wall. To make the goal happen, you need to break it up into pieces and start doing them. For example, you might add the following entries into specific days in your agenda:

- March 15—Take my daughter alone for a walk.
- April 10—Buy the book called *P.E.T.* on how to improve parenting skills.
- May 12—Look for a parenting support group.
- May 13—Ask Margarita (who has great kids) for tips on parenting.
- June 16—Encourage Matt to talk to me about his goals.
- June 18—Ask my mother to help one hour a week so I have time for myself to recharge.

If the goals are less about personal improvement and more about a project, then you have to set deadlines for the project. I have done this for several projects, and posted the dates up right in front of me in my bedroom. So, if you plan to open your own café, your entries in your agenda might look like this:

- March 10—Talk to Mark, who owns a restaurant, about the cost of buying equipment.

- April—Try to find out the cost of leases on Bank Street.
- May—Talk to Lisa about financing this project.
- September—Take a management course at ABC University.
- October—Learn how to prepare a business plan. Etc. . . .

Breaking up a goal into achievable steps is key. But we cannot forget the effect of belief on our goals. Jane Ogden, Ph.D., a health psychologist at Guys Kings and St. Thomas's School of Medicine in London, studied women whose goal was to lose weight. What she found is that the women who believed their weight problem was due to their own behavior, such as their eating habit and exercise habits, were more successful at losing weight then those thought the problem was due to external factors such as genes or metabolism. "If a person believes their heart attack was caused by over-exertion, then they are unlikely to follow advice to exercise as this solution does not match their cause. Similarly, if a person believes their obesity is caused by their metabolism or genetics, they are unlikely to change their diet."[58]

Remember our discussions about the importance of your beliefs, on opening the door to possibilities and on learned helplessness? To achieve your goals, whether about parenting, life, work, or friendships, you will need to align your belief system with your goals, be open to possibilities around you, and see that your actions do matter. You do have some control, and you are not helpless.

Once you are on your way, another great tactic to increasing the likelihood of achieving your goals is going public with them. I don't mean on a loudspeaker or in the newspaper. I mean telling friends, family, or colleagues what you're up to. It's easier to go back on your word when no one knows about it. It's harder when people will hold you to it.

The other fascinating thing that happens when you announce your goals is that people ask you about them, keeping you motivated. I told many single moms that I wanted to write a book about single motherhood, and each time I saw them, they'd ask me about it. I would tell them about my progress, we would often exchange more ideas, and this helped keep me on track. It's an upward spiral.

STRATEGY #20

Visualize

We've all heard of the term "visualizing" our goals, but what does it really mean? It means seeing images or movies in our minds, imagining. When making a mental picture of something, think about the event as if it were really happening in the way that you would like it to happen—a kind of positive daydreaming. If you need to give a talk, you rehearse it in your head, picturing yourself standing there, speaking. People are listening. Perhaps a few people congratulate you afterwards for your interesting speech. If you have to go to a job interview, imagine yourself walking in the door, shaking hands with a smile, and sitting comfortably and being yourself. Imagine feeling confident.

According to a *Psychology Today* article published in 2000, "Some Olympians say 'mental management' accounts for 90% of their success." And, "studies by the U.S. Olympic Training Center show that 94% of coaches use mental rehearsal for training and competition."[59]

When we visualize something, whether it's a ski trail or a hurdle, your brain starts to feel like you actually did it. The belief that it is achievable becomes ingrained. Consider the following story about the value of positive visualization from an article called "The Gold Medal Mind" in *Psychology Today*. Kathy Ann Colin was able to overcome injuries, and deal with college and unexpected family events to become the No. 1 kayaker in the United States. She describes how she visualizes gliding though the water as she lies in bed at night. "I focus on the feel of the boat and on my paddling. I am in the race. I get nervous energy. My muscles are triggered as I simulate a stroke in my mind. The boat is picking up; it's gliding and I'm gliding with it." During warm-ups on the water, Colin's visualizations are key: 'I'll hold a stop watch and imagine the start. My strategy is to figure out the number of strokes I need to win. I tell myself I want to get 152 then I make the plan. I know exactly where I'll be when I stop, and I'll be within a second of my goal. So when the race comes, there's nothing new."[60]

Some books claim that visualizing events will simply make them happen, as if the universe will simply work all its magic to make what you visualized happen. I'm not sure it's such a straightforward process. Visualizing getting a gold medal in kayaking is not, in and of itself, going to get you the gold medal no matter what universal forces come into play. But visualization can be an important *part* of the process to increasing your chances at the gold medal for several reasons:

- It breaks down fear of failure, or other fears associated with the topic.
- It makes you open to the idea and belief in your vision (being closed to an idea definitely hurts the possibility of it happening).
- It motivates you to make it happen since you have visualized the positive feelings associated with getting it.
- It keeps you focused on the right track, as previously discussed in the focus section.

Take some time to drift off during your car ride, before going to sleep, in your shower, on what you'd like to achieve in your life. Visualize it. And visualize it often. This will tackle fear, make you open, motivate you and keep you focused. This will spark creative thoughts in your mind about ideas on how to make it happen.

But then it's time to do the work. Write down what you want. Now cut it up into 5–10 or 20 tasks and start to do it! You'd be amazed how taking the first step can start to make you feel like it's a reality. Just take that first step!

STRATEGY #21

Make Some Friends

Feeling close to people is one of the *most meaningful factors* in increasing your happiness. How close you are with friends and family, and what your relationship is with your co-workers and neighbors are key factors for increasing your happiness.

Friends are crucial for sharing problems. Credit counselors often tell people, "The only thing that hiding your problems accomplishes is making sure no one helps you with them." I don't know why so many people conceal their problems as if in shame. There is a real comfort in being authentic in expressing your experiences, and accepting the truth and reality of them instead of hiding and faking. And you'd be absolutely surprised at how helpful people can be when they know you need support or help. Why not mention to people that you've had a difficult week, or that you are struggling with an issue? Many people will respond to this and even offer help. This will also encourage them to share their problems with you. This will cultivate your relationships and take them beyond the superficial "How are you?" "Fine and you?" "Fine, thanks." Ask for help—everyone will come out ahead!

For those who have strained family relations or no family, you'll be pleased to know that in *100 Simple Secrets of Happy People*, David Niven found research showing that "there were no differences in overall happiness between those who mainly relied upon friends for companionship and those who mainly relied upon family. People have the power to create happiness from the relationships available to them and do not need all their relationships to fit an ideal image."[61]

DOES TALKING ABOUT CONCERNS HELP?

Did you ever wonder why we always feel better after talking to our girlfriends? A University of Michigan study has identified the likely cause: "Feeling emotionally close to a friend increases levels of the hormone progesterone, helping to boost well-being and reduce anxiety and stress." Lead researcher Stephanie Brown says: "These links may help us understand why people in close relationships are happier, healthier, and live longer than those who are socially isolated."[62]

In order to bounce back from your downs, it's important to have friends to share the experience, especially if they can help you learn and grow. It's also great to have people around to share the good experiences. When Ed Diener and Martin Seligman studied hundreds of students to see what the happiest 10 percent have in common, they found that it was those who spent the least time alone and the most time socializing.[63]

So undoubtedly, to improve our level of well-being, we need to cultivate our relationships with the people around us. You can start with your children, by having real conversations, discussing your child's points of view, or going for walks instead of simply dropping them off at endless activities. Doing simple things together will allow you to bond.

But for most of us, this is simply not enough. We need adults in our lives, whether it's new partners or friends. Although most of us have some acquaintances, friends are so much harder to find. With friends there is a true emotional connection. Many of us know that some of our "friendships" are fake and fragile. Some people are just around for the good times and are not going to be there for the long haul. Although you might interact and have a social relationship with some people everyday, at work for example, this does not necessarily make that person a friend. Being on someone's list on MySpace, Flickr, or Facebook is also not an indicator. Many people admit they have only one or two friends, *if any*.

Some of you, like myself, did not have much of a social network during marriage or when we found ourselves as single parents. Many women in bad marriages end up isolated for various reasons. Our individualistic society does not help. If you were like me, without any true friends, you will need to start somewhere. Don't give up! It is never too late to find friends. Join a single-parent club that does activities, hiking, and lectures on weekends. Make extra efforts to form relationships. Try to get together with people or invite them over. Try to meet people whenever the situation permits. Try not to be too picky at first. Some people can be good for you for certain needs and other people for different needs. You don't need to like everything about a person to have them in your life.

And try asking for help from people as a way to make friends. Needing each other is a fantastic way to cultivate a relationship. For example, your neighbor helps you with something, maybe watching your kids, and you reciprocate, maybe picking up some groceries. In North America we are often used to getting bus service, grocery service, taxi service, delivery service, and many other services so that friends are less needed for these types of things. Try the old-fashioned route for a while. The benefits are enormous.

I remember doing something that people rarely do these days because someone suggested I try the "asking for help" concept in order to cultivate friendships. I went to my neighbor whom I barely knew, and asked if she had sugar because my son was sick and I didn't want to take him out in the winter to the grocery store to get some. She happily gave me some, and we started a nice conversation. We got to know each other better, and she didn't hesitate to ask me if she could borrow my fridge some time later when she was organizing a party upstairs and her fridge was too full. You'd be surprised how people actually like to help each other but are not always given the opportunity to do so. Sometimes you need to start it.

Liz (not her real name) went through a long and difficult divorce, during which both her parents passed away so it was very difficult for her. But she knew that she needed support. "You need to find it sometimes." She said, "You can't sit at home in the chair and say 'Oh maybe someone will call me.' You need to go and reach out and not be afraid to reach out."

STRATEGY #22

And Finally, Be Kind to Others

Some of us may have religious or moral reasons for being kind and good. But science has discovered that there is another good reason for being altruistic. David Niven's research shows that "Volunteers, on average, are twice as likely to feel happy with themselves as non-volunteers."[64] They feel like they have purpose and feel appreciated. "Life satisfaction was found to improve 24% with the level of altruistic activity."[65]

Many of us might feel like we are already doing enough for others. We are taking care of our children, our friend's children, our parents, and others. But in some ways, assuming we don't feel taken advantage of, this is good for us!

Stephanie Brown, a social psychologist at the University of Michigan's Institute for Social Research, found that when it comes to social support, it might be better to give than to receive. She conducted a study of more than 400 older married couples and found that those who said they provided emotional support to their spouses or practical support such as helping with errands, and child care to friends and relatives "reduced their chances of dying by between 40 and 60 percent in a five-year period."[66] Receiving support had no such effect on mortality. It is possible that giving increases positive emotions, which in turn reduces the negative effects of negative emotion on one's health.[67]

Why is giving and being kind good for us? "Giving makes you feel good about yourself," says Christopher Peterson, Ph.D., and professor of psychology at University of Colorado. "When you're volunteering, you're distracting yourself from your own existence, and that's beneficial. More fuzzily, giving puts meaning into your life. You have a sense of purpose because you matter to someone else." Virtually all the happiness exercises being tested by positive psychologists, he told *Time* magazine, make people feel more connected to others.[68]

For those of us whose hands already seem full, I challenge you to do even more. You can do small acts of kindness that do not require time or money. You can let a pedestrian pass by when you're driving. You can open the door for an elderly person. You can also encourage your children to do the same. Good deeds can directly cause an increase in well-being.

Stanford University psychologist and author of *How of Happiness* Sonja Lyubomirsky tested the connection between kindness and happiness by asking students to do five random acts of kindness a week of their choice. It could be anything from giving money to a homeless person to washing someone's dishes. As you can imagine, the study showed that doing good deeds resulted in an increase in well-being.[69] "There are a lot of positive social consequences to being kind—other people appreciate you, they're grateful and they might reciprocate," Lyubomirsky says. All of these responses, she is quoted as saying in *Psychology Today*, are likely to make your happiness cup run over.[70]

If time is a factor, and I'm sure it is for most of you, then volunteering or acts of kindness can take a smaller scale and not take time. Jonathan Haidt, a University of Virginia psychologist and author of *The Happiness Hypothesis*, suggests focusing on doing actions that strengthen existing social ties and relationships, such as driving to visit your grandmother.[71] You will see that these details get repaid, and you will feel happier too! It's all up to you now!

> "This is the beginning of a new day. You have been given this day to use as you will. You can waste it or use it for good. What you do today is important because you are exchanging a day of your life for it. When tomorrow comes, this day will be gone forever; in its place is something that you have left behind . . . let it be something good."
>
> —Author unknown

SECTION 5

The Single Mother in Charge

Her Power

We need to be the change we wish to see in the world.

—Mahatma Gandhi[1]

There are those who would label single mothers as the humans with the least power in society. I would argue that we are among the *most* powerful people in the world. The reason is simple. We have a great deal of influence on the next generation since we are raising them, and doing so mostly on our own.

And we are more numerous than ever. In the United States, there are over 8 million households run by single mothers. That translates to about 25 percent of families with children under 18.[2]

But this figure fails to portray the whole story. Although during any given year there may be a certain number of single mothers, if you actually look at the *lifetime* of women, the numbers are much greater. Given the current divorce rate, I suspect that *most* mothers spend time as single mothers *at some point in their lives* (even if we don't all do so in the same year).

As for the children, these figures do not acknowledge single motherhood after children turn 18, and they do not relay the fact that most children will spend time in a single-parent home *at some point in their childhoods*. These figures also do not include *de facto* single mothers: women who live within an intact marriage but who are, for all intents and purposes, single mothers. Many of us felt like single mothers before becoming "single mothers." Finally, these figures do not include mothers who continue to take on the primary care of their children even after they get remarried. We are more numerous than it might first appear.

So how can we use our power? Once we have emptied our cup from all the negative emotion, and used some of the strategies in Section 4 to be happier and more balanced, we can become better people and better mothers. We are now in a position to use our power as single mothers to pass on some of this wisdom and raise happier and more responsible children. Our cup is now filled with some positive ingredients and we can let that spill out to the world around us—especially to our children. And we are in a perfect position to do so.

Kerrie (not her real name), a divorced mother of two, thinks that had she remained married, her kids would never have known who *she* really was, and would have suffered for that loss. By being with another partner, we tend to compromise our views and adopt a more "shared" view of how to raise children. Some of us may even accept our partner's methods completely in order to keep peace in the home. This may not be the case for everyone, but it certainly is for some. In those situations, it is possible that the child would never have known our true views and we would not have parented with the same freedom.

I know I play the most important role in teaching my son values like honesty, respecting women and humans in general, including himself, the importance of healthy habits, using our strengths for positive purposes, and many other aspects of living a decent and happy life.

This doesn't mean that he doesn't get other viewpoints from many others in his life. It's just that I have the privilege of having a primary role in influencing him. I doubt that this would have occurred had I remained married since I had a hard time being completely myself in my marriage. Once I was on my own, I felt the freedom to develop my own parenting style. The result is that I am now in a very powerful position—a position to influence the next generation, albeit one person at a time. We can make a difference and change the world, one child at time.

As mothers, whether we are married or not, we can use this power of influence to improve our society and reduce conflict in our world. Is it possible that, at least in some circumstances, single motherhood might have a positive impact on children and society? Many women I spoke to think that their children are likely to turn out to be "better people" because they were raised by a single mother than they would have been had they been raised in an intact home, especially if the level of conflict was high in that intact home.

Studies have confirmed the importance of the mother's influence. They have also played a role in dispelling some myths about the impact of single motherhood on children's development and education.

Henry Ricciuti, a professor emeritus of human development in the College of Human Ecology at Cornell University, has found that single parenthood, in and of itself, does not appear to be a risk factor for a child's performance or behavior.[3] He says, "Overall, we find little or no evidence of systematic negative effects of single parenthood on children, regardless of how long they have lived with a single parent during the previous six years," he says.[4] What mattered most in this study was the mother's education, ability level, and coping skills and, to a lesser extent, family income and quality of the home environment. Whether the family was white, black, or Hispanic, this study showed a consistent connection between these maternal attributes and a child's school performance and behavior.[5]

Other research also confirms that it is the parenting style rather than family structure that the main determinant of the well-being of adolescents.[6]

The Single Mother in Charge knows she is powerful and that her influence is critical for her child's development, and she uses this power wisely and responsibly.

Her Role

I love this description of a female tiger's parenting skills I found online and often use the analogy with my friends to give us strength.

A tigress is one of the most perfect mothers to inhabit the planet. She takes on the responsibilities of every aspect in the development of her young into independent adults. To the female cubs she passes on the methods of raising cubs. She teaches all her young the methods of stalking and outwitting their prey. Her patience and tolerance is infinite. The cubs jump on her head, bite at her purposely flicking tail and play endlessly all around her but she patiently puts up with it all. After the suckling period, she has the added burden of providing kills for feeding her cubs too. She trains her cubs to stay hidden from the dangers of the jungle while she is away hunting. She is also very careful and regular with frequent changes of their den for the same reason. She gently carries each cub from the neck to the new den, however far it may be. Once the cubs are old enough to start accompanying her on small walks into her territory, the shifting of dens becomes less frequent. She sometimes has to take on other tigers and tigresses to protect her young. After first teaching her cubs the art of hunting, she is known to actually provide live prey at times for practicing and perfecting their techniques. She teaches them what not to fear and what to avoid. The latter being mainly man. She allows a hierarchy to develop among the cubs. The dominant male cub always has the first go at a fresh kill.

She teaches them how to adhere to the territorial regulations set by all tigers. Until they are old enough to fend for themselves, she takes care of all her cubs' needs and requirements. Once they are capable of being independent individuals, mostly when they are past the age of 2 years, she encourages them to move out and find their own territories and position in the jungle."[7]

Her Instincts

I read a wonderful book once called *Protecting the Gift* by Gavin de Becker about protecting your kids. De Becker, the security expert who also wrote the *Gift of Fear*, offers advice on recognizing signs of sexual abuse, choosing a babysitter, and how to teach children about potential risks, including talking to strangers.

His angle is sometimes different from what we are accustomed to. For example, rather than teaching your children *not* to talk to strangers (since they see us speak to strangers all the time such as bus drivers, dry cleaners, clerks, new neighbors, etc.) he *encourages* the interaction. He suggests teaching our kids to practice talking to strangers, then discussing the interactions with them. This helps develop their "gut feelings" and their ability to discern normal from unusual behavior, he writes. For example, when your children are of a certain age, you might tell them to go ask a person the time while you're at the mall. Then when they come back, you can discuss what seemed strange or nice about a person instead of insisting that they just be "polite." I highly recommend this book to every parent.

What stuck with me the most from this book was the author's absolute insistence on trusting your instincts when it comes to dealing with your children. He continually stressed that denying and ignoring intuition is often the biggest mistake that a parent can make in protecting their children.

As women, we are taught to be "nice." And as a result, as we discussed earlier, we sometimes rationalize away our gut instincts. For example, if our instincts tell us our male cousin acts a bit strange with little girls, we might dismiss this with "He probably just likes children a lot." If our gut tells us that the swimming teacher doesn't seem to supervise the kids in the pool well, we might dismiss this as "Oh, he must know what he's doing since he's done this for 30 years." If our feelings tell us the babysitter is acting unusual when we come home, we might say, "Oh, but Susan has been using her for years and says she's wonderful, so I must be imagining things."

Why do we do this? Why do we doubt our instincts and judgment? Think back to when the last time your gut was telling you something was clearly wrong and you ignored this and tried to find rational excuses. What happened?

Rita (not her real name) recalls the night before her wedding. She remembers that there was some problem with the hotel and how she first saw her fiancé displaying signs of aggressiveness. Although he didn't physically abuse her, she felt he was demeaning and aggressive in a way she had not seen him before. She told him she no longer wanted to get married and he spent the whole night, until 7:00 a.m. the next morning, discussing why she should. Of course, they got married and four years later, Rita found herself in the kitchen with her toddler under the table, terrified because his father was running at his mother with a knife. Rita managed to fight him off, and to end the "relationship."

Since reading these two books, I never ignore my gut, especially when it comes to my son. In fact, I'm convinced that it is one of the most powerful tools I have. This does not mean I don't take the time to reflect or sit on something. But if my instinct is persistently saying something, I respect it. Even if I can't pinpoint the exact "reasonable explanation" for my decision, I will not be embarrassed to say that "this is what my intuition tells me."

I see single mothers like lions or tigers taking care of our young. We have instincts and they are there for a reason. Why ignore them? Sometimes it is impossible to actually pinpoint why our gut tells us someone is behaving strangely. Maybe they looked at us in a funny way; maybe it was some gesture. The exact rationale is not always obvious. We have so much accumulated data in our brains, and we cannot always discern or identify the exact details that have led to our conclusions. But if it results in us having a "funny feeling" about it, it's for a reason! And let's not ignore that anymore.

Our instincts are useful not only for cases involving danger or abuse, but also for the smaller or more subtle decisions. Many people can offer advice about how to act or raise your children (as I am doing in this book). But the truth is, you are the only person who really

> "Believe nothing because someone else believes it. But believe only what you yourself judge to be true."
>
> —Buddha

knows all the facts and context of your life and those of your children! Many things people say might sound "reasonable" and it might be hard to discount them. But you are the only person who knows the whole situation. And you might not even be able to rationally vocalize all these nuances and the millions of little bits of accumulated information in your brain. But you know all this information, and your child, and this is why you are in the best position to make decisions based on your authentic and instinctive feeling about situations. If you end up making a mistake, that is OK. This mistake will be yours and you will learn from it. This is better than doing something someone else told you to do that ends up being wrong for you and your family.

I don't always end up knowing whether my gut was right or wrong, and I imagine it is wrong sometimes, but this does not dissuade me from continuing to respect my instinct out of principle! So please respect yourself; that's more important than anything you might read in this book.

As a female in charge of her young, you are well equipped for the task. You have been given the privilege of being your child's first and most important teacher. You have been given maternal instincts, and I think these should be embraced.

I will now share with you some strategies that have helped me to raise a happier child. Of course, these won't guarantee that your child (or mine) will be happy; rather they are strategies that I think can increase your child's overall well-being compared to what might be if these strategies were not used. I hope my experiences may be useful to you, but I encourage you to keep respecting your own intuition about how to raise *your* child.

Her Influence

When my son was eight, his teacher asked the class to promise that they will read every single day for a certain amount of time. She asked every child in class to raise their hand and promise to do so. My son and one other child refused to raise their hand. He explained to the teacher that he sometimes has activities after school and doesn't want to promise something that he might not do every single day. He was yelled at, and reprimanded and a note was sent home for me to sign. He came home in tears, but after I heard the story, I gave him a big hug and a big congratulations!! I told him it was one of the proudest moments of my life. He had the courage to be truthful unlike most of the other children who probably just agreed to avoid getting into trouble. I was so proud of him. I told him I would not sign the letter, and that he can tell the teacher the following:

First, that his mother was very proud of him for not lying. And second, to see if he could find a solution with the teacher to do necessary readings on a weekly basis instead of promising to read every single day.

Lo and behold, the teacher never questioned him the next day. (By the way, this story does not change the fact that I love my son's school and his teachers and am very grateful to them all.)

Does this mean that you should teach your children to defy their teachers or to refuse homework? Absolutely not!! That is not the point of this story.

The point of this story is to show you that I consider *myself* to be the primary teacher of my son and will not simply get nervous into giving up this role. Schools and teachers cannot impose their views on how we should raise our children. They can set rules and consequences at the school, and we might have to live with those, but they cannot change how we think or how we choose to raise our children. We are in charge.

Most parents know they are in charge for some things. They are comfortable taking charge when it comes to *physical* danger or *physical* well-being of their children. The use of car seats is not negotiable nor is jumping into the pool at the age of two unattended. But it is not only a child's *physical* well-being that needs protection but also things that affect their *emotional or general well-being*. Yes, a car seat is important, but so is good nutrition, sleep, and not watching too much TV. So is feeling safe and secure, having space to grow, make mistakes, and build self esteem. I would argue that it's not only our role to take charge of these issues, but our responsibility!

Being in charge does not mean having an "I'm the boss" attitude or being a dictator. Being too authoritarian, setting strict rules to try to keep order, and exercising strong control lead to children not thinking for themselves. Children of authoritarian parents have been shown to end up rebellious and lacking in self-esteem. As kids grow, they need to learn to make their own decisions even if it means that they will make mistakes on the way. They need to progressively control their environment, in order to avoid later problems associated with learned helplessness.

Being in charge means that I do not simply *hand over* the responsibility for raising my child to others—or simply stand by if I think my son's education is lacking in some way. It means being *attentive* to his needs.

Being in charge includes expressing warmth and affection. It means listening to and understanding the child, and giving the child freedom and space to grow. It means encouraging independence and independent decision making, even making mistakes. And it also means being true to your values and explaining why you might feel a certain way about certain things.

Taking charge might mean imposing consequences in some instances, having conversations in others, ignoring behavior on occasion, or listening to your child's concerns. It might mean making efforts to improve the relationship, expressing frustrations, or getting help. Being in charge simply means that it's your place and role to deal with it. I consider it my role to be a positive influence to my son, whether directly or indirectly.

I'll give you an example of indirectly taking charge. My son's feet grow at a remarkable rate, and I feel like I buy new shoes for him every few months. One day, my son told me that his shoes felt a bit tight, again. I told him I'd buy him another pair of shoes in the next few days. He wasn't too happy that he had to go to school with slightly tight shoes. A few days later I bought him his new shoes. But I *also* bought the movie *Children of Heaven*, a 1997 Iranian movie about two young children who had to share their shoes knowing there was no money to replace the one that was lost. Roger Ebert's review in the *Chicago Sun-Times* called it "very nearly a perfect movie for children" that "lacks the cynicism and smart-mouth attitudes of so much American entertainment for kids and glows with a kind of good-hearted purity."[8] This is how I took charge in this instance. I decided to be the one in charge of influencing my son's value system instead of simply going with the flow of society. You will have to see the movie to understand the full impact of my approach.

These examples might be about my son choosing to be truthful, or other times when I've supported his judgment, or about having slightly tight shoes for a day, but I have taken this approach with regard to a multitude of other issues. Whether it comes to respecting others, TV, video games, or education, I do not simply go with society's flow about these issues but actually take charge of trying to influence my son in a positive way. Barack Obama's mother was 19 when she had him, and her husband left when she was 21. In the preface of his book he wrote of his single mother who gave him love, education, and hope, "What is best in me I owe to her."[9]

I think as mothers we need to take ownership of setting the tone for our children's behavior and attitudes. I think this is particularly important for single mothers. For some reason people feel more at liberty to offer advice and try to control our kids when they know there is no man in the home. It is very difficult to keep feeling in charge of our children's well-being, but I think it's important to do so. There is a very subtle difference between people offering to help and participate with your children—which most of us usually welcome—and people imposing themselves on you and your children with a sense of entitlement while treating you as weak, messed-up, irresponsible, or incapable.

The Single Mother in Charge knows that she is in charge of her children and is not afraid of this role. She has the power to delegate, authorize others, and allow others to influence and communicate with her children. But she keeps her position. Where there is a void in the lessons her children need, she takes charge and tries to fill that void.

Whether it's about values or math, we can make a difference and fill the gaps. If the school or their math teacher does not teach well in your opinion, then teach your child math. I know an amazing single mother who was able to completely reverse and conquer her child's belief that he is incapable of doing math. If the school doesn't teach reading well, buy your child more books, or take them out from the library. If your child seems to need some time alone or unstructured time, take him or her out of school for a day to give your child some space to breath. We can teach our children manners, respect for others, how to be a friend, how to be strong, how to solve problems. As mothers, we can use our power to shape future generations. And remember, our parenting affects not only our children but the way our children will parent our grandchildren![10]

Take charge of your children! As a mother, we are like tigers. Not only in a protective manner, but also in terms of the power we have to change the world. We can influence them, particularly by setting a good example. Use the power of single motherhood!

One good mother is worth a hundred schoolmasters.

—George Herbert[11]

Her Expectations

In Section 1, we discussed the power our beliefs can have over our lives. But what about the beliefs we have about our children?

In 1968, Harvard professor Robert Rosenthal conducted a famous experiment with elementary school children from 18 classrooms. The study randomly chose 20 percent of the children from each room and falsely told the teachers that these students were tested and found to be "intellectual bloomers" and "on the brink of intellectual growth and development." In other words, they told the teachers that these children were geniuses. At the end of the year, the students who were *expected* to excel by the teachers showed significantly greater intellectual growth than did those in the control group. They even scored higher on IQ tests than other students. In other words, when teachers expect their students to do well, they do. This "self-fulfilling prophecy" is also commonly known as the Pygmalion Effect.[12]

As your children's primary teacher, ask yourself what expectations you have of your "student." These expectations can have a profound effect on your child. The implication of the Pygmalion Effect is that the performance of our children may depend very much on what we expect and believe about our children. Think about what you expect from your children, even if you don't openly communicate it. Write down those beliefs to see if you sincerely believe them. Seeing them on paper somehow gives a new perspective to things. You might be limiting yourself and your kids without realizing it.

And be especially careful about labeling your children, a surefire way to create beliefs about your children. There is a difference between a mother telling her child "you are so stupid" and "I really felt what you did was dangerous." There's a difference between saying "your room is a mess" and "you are such a slob." Even in the heat of the moment, humiliating or insulting words should be avoided.

If you call your child "bad," "shy," "clumsy," "stubborn," "mean," "stupid," or "a liar," they are more likely to grow up to be one of those things than if you hadn't used that terminology. When a child is labeled, then their *belief* is that it is "innate," biological, genetic, and *unchangeable*. Conversely, if it was a behavior you found unacceptable, then the message is that it is within their control to change that behavior. And if you catch yourself making mistakes, then, once things have calmed down, talk about it with your child. Explain why the behavior was unacceptable to you and take back what you misstated.

What beliefs are you fostering in your children as they grow? I asked my son at age nine what he thinks makes kids confident. He said, "If you convince them they can do it when they are not sure about something they are gonna do. And if you relax them before doing something." In other words, if you believe in them, they will believe in themselves.

The Single Mother in Charge knows how her beliefs can affect those of her children. Use your power as a single mother to raise the best child you can. Question your expectations and beliefs about your children. What do you believe your child is capable of? What do you expect from them? What do they believe about themselves as a result?

The key is not just to tell children you expect something or that you believe they can do it, but rather to *really* expect it and believe in the child. You might not even need to say it when this is the case. They'll know.

Jogging with my son the other day, he wanted to stop and complained of being tired and his feet hurting. I told him we could stop and walk the rest of the way, but I also told him that I believed he could manage to jog all the way home if he wanted to—and I truly believed it. He paused, walked for a few moments, and then decided to jog... then he sprinted at the end (and beat me, with a big smile on his face)!

Do be careful about setting expectations since they can also be harmful, create too much pressure and be counterproductive. They need to be appropriate for the age, personality, and life circumstances that the child might be going though at any given time. If you know your child is going through a difficult time, you might need to modify the expectations for some time. Expectations need to be reassessed on a constant basis. If you see that your expectations are too high, or not necessary or important, then they might need to be reduced or eliminated about certain things. And try to limit expectations to things that *matter*. It's a work in progress, but if you take the time to at least think about them you are more likely to be on the right track. I hope I am.

Her Strength

When my son was two years old, a friend of mine started talking to me about the importance of being a strong individual in order to give a sense of security to my son. I didn't quite understand, back then, how my being too "soft" would lead to my son feeling insecure. I couldn't see the connection.

One day I went to the mall with another mom who had a child the same age as mine. I had, by this time, started trying not to be a mother who is afraid, insecure or "wrapped around their child's finger," and was instead working toward becoming a parent who was balanced and in charge of my little household. This does not mean I wasn't loving. It just means that I was trying to put reasonable boundaries on acceptable behavior. Meanwhile, I could see that my girlfriend was still being dragged around by the whim of her two-year-old.

I sensed that my friend's little son could tell that I was the "stronger" mom since my son was not allowed to dictate my every move or succeed at getting things through tantrums.

About an hour later, my friend's son fell and got hurt right next to me and his mother. But he immediately turned to *me, instead of his mother*, with his hands up for "saving" and comfort.

At that moment, I realized the connection between the strength of a mother and the sense of security this can give to a child. The same strength that you portray by not being a pushover with your children, is same strength that they feel they can seek when they need help or answers. Who would *you* turn to when you need help? The wimpy adult or the solid adult? Which one would make you feel safe and secure—the pushover or the strong one?

If your child sees you as a strong person, they will trust that you will catch them when they fall, trust your judgment when you tell them that they can climb higher, believe you when you tell them that you will handle problems and speak on their behalf when needed, etc. This makes them feel more secure.

Become a tiger with your children. This does not mean that you cannot be loving and soft. There are plenty of occasions where this is exactly the thing the child needs. And it certainly doesn't mean being nasty or aggressive. Strength is internal and calm. It means building your inside, your strong mind, and taking charge when necessary. Kids feel more secure and confident when the parent is strong.

My strong mind comes primarily from my martial arts class. It makes me feel stronger physically and mentally, and more able to tackle my world. I recommend kickboxing or martial arts classes to any single mother to build her confidence and strength—not the aerobics-type classes offered at some gyms, but rather a class taught by a trained martial artist. Even if you go once a week, I think it can do wonders for many women. Only once you've done these kinds of classes for some time will you realize that it is more about strengthening the mind than the body. You will inevitably learn how to calm the mind in the face of challenges, fear, and adversity. How to handle things. How to learn to master yourself.

If this is not for you, then maybe you can build your strength through a helpful friend, a support group, meditation, or reading inspiring biographies of other women you admire. Whatever method you use, try to notice the difference in your children when they feel they have a solid parent with them. Notice how you might walk differently when you feel strong. Notice your confidence level. And of course, for those of you with daughters, notice that you are setting an example of strong and independent womanhood for them. This positive feeling will carry over throughout their lives.

Her Wisdom

I remember one of the first snowfalls in Montreal in 2005—the whole city was white and beautiful. When I picked up my son and his friend from school they were wide-eyed and excited, immediately jumping in the snow to make snow angels and throwing snowballs at each other.

Immediately, a mother standing nearby said something I thought I'd never hear. She told the three kids she was with, "Do not throw snowballs at people, only to the ground." The three kids then had to throw the snowballs at the ground and not at each other! It was a pretty sad sight. I wondered if this is what life had come to in our over-protective society. When I recounted this story to a friend of mine, he recommended that I should have thrown a snowball at that mom. (I'm not sure that would have been such a good idea.)

I recall a similarly strange experience at a private beach not far from my city. There was a beautiful tree there that I encouraged my son, then three, to try to climb. I was quickly met by security who told me that the rules on that beach were "no climbing trees" due to potential injuries and liability!

We all know that snowballs and climbing trees can lead to injury, as can many other activities, but isn't it also important to weigh the risk of injury against what is going to be lost if these activities are *not* done? The Single Mother in Charge knows that she sometimes needs to let her kids stumble to learn.

Take the simple example of walking on top of a low brick wall. When a child climbs a wall, they might fall. But they might also become better climbers, thereby reducing their risk of injury in the future, develop better balance, increase self-esteem through achievement and challenge, and get some exercise.

As parents we need to not only be aware of the child's "physical" well-being in terms of safety, but also weigh other aspects of well-being—like having a sense of accomplishment and self-mastery—which sometimes requires taking some risks and facing challenges. When things are too easy for children, you are not doing the children a favor by depriving them of the privilege of struggle. This doesn't build resilience.

Does this mean we should encourage risky behavior? Of course not. The idea is to consider the whole picture when permitting or refraining a child from doing something. Consider the risks, but *also* give some value to potential long-term benefits, and *then* make a decision. Consider being less overprotective—for their own good.

Lenore Skenazy has taken these thoughts to heart, and her "free-range parenting" concept is catching on. Skenazy became famous when she allowed her nine-year old son to ride the New York subway alone, then wrote about it in her column. Skenazy was branded "America's Worst Mom," which she doesn't seem to mind, and she is now inspired to convince parents to stop going crazy worrying and to give their children some freedom.[13] She thinks our fears of our children being kidnapped or killed if they do something as simple as biking alone to the park are completely exaggerated.[14] Because we are constantly bombarded with information on everything we should fear, we have become neurotic even though, she says, we live in one of the safest times, statistically.[15]

Many parents these days try to prevent their children from having any difficulties. We equip them with the latest protective gear, they play only in matted or rubber playgrounds, to avoid even skinned knees, and we prevent them from being exposed to any bacteria. And we try to solve all their problems, even small ones. They are living, what Hara Estroff Marano, author of *A Nation of Wimps*, calls "wholly sanitized childhoods."[16]

I, like most parents, don't like to see my child fail, in pain or feel sad, but I can also see the downside of this approach—that it can sometimes be counterproductive to protect kids from these experiences.

"Kids need to feel badly sometimes," says child psychologist David Elkind, professor at Tufts University and author of *The Hurried Child*. "We learn through experience and we learn through bad experiences. Through failure we learn how to cope."[17] Kids today are told that they can do anything, be anything, that everyone's a winner and nobody loses. There are even soccer clubs for kids where there is no score keeping during the match. I suppose this is done to protect the children from feeling like losers. But how will this prepare them for life in any way? These messages of omnipotence are creating children with too high a sense of entitlement.

Marano writes further in *A Nation of Wimps* that "messing up, however, even in the playground, is wildly out of style. Although error and experimentation are the true mothers of success, parents are taking pains to remove failure from the equation."[18] She thinks that when we try to make everything easy for our children in the short run, we might be making things harder for them in the long run. Plus, we might be depriving our "children of meaning and a shot at deep satisfaction."[19]

She goes on to say: "But taking all the discomfort, the disappointment and even the play out of development, especially while increasing pressure for success, turns out to be misguided by just about 180 degrees. With few challenges all their own, through which to sharpen their instincts and identities, kids are unable to forge their creative adaptations to the normal vicissitudes of life. That not only makes them extraordinarily risk-averse, it makes them psychologically fragile. In the process they're robbed of identity, meaning and a sense of mastery, which underlies real happiness. Forget, too, about perseverance, not simply a moral virtue but a necessary life skill. These features have turned out to be the spreading psychic fault lines of twenty-first-century youth. Whether we're aware of it or not, we're on our way to creating a nation of wimps."[20]

Overprotectiveness can also creep up in your attitude regarding your children's illnesses and injuries. How do you react when there is an injury or illness? And how does that affect them? Do you remember the section on the power of belief discussed in Section 1? Consider this study from the early 1980s in which 34 college students were told an electric current would be passed through their heads and that they might experience headaches as a result. "Though *not a single volt* of current was used, more than two-thirds of the students reported headaches!"[21]

Remember the placebo and nocebo effects also from Section 1? Japanese researchers, Drs. Ikemi and Nakagawa, studied schoolboys who reported being allergic to a Japanese tree whose leaves produce a rash similar to poison ivy. They brushed one arm of each boy with harmless chestnut leaves, and the other arm with poisonous leaves. But the boys were told that the researchers had done the *exact opposite*.[22]

Can you guess what happened? The physical symptoms matched with the symptoms that were suggested! "All 13 subjects displayed a skin reaction to the harmless leaves (the placebo), but only two reacted to the poisonous leaves."[23] Isn't it amazing that rashes appeared on the arms where there was no poison? Isn't it also amazing that skin reactions were prevented simply because the children were convinced that the substance was harmless?

Think about these studies when you react to your child falling, having a cold, or anything else. You can be the source of the placebo or nocebo effect!

Her Empathy

Acceptance is probably one of the most important components of making a child feel well and loved, and ultimately psychologically healthy. It is also one of the concepts that has been and continues to be the most difficult for me to fully grasp. It is deeper and more complicated than simply telling a child you love them from time to time.

When a child feels accepted, *as is*, they feel loved, which can actually promote their healthy growth and self-actualization. If you do not have a healthy level of acceptance of your child, they are likely to have lower self-esteem and well-being problems.

Acceptance of a child can be communicated in several ways. One way is by not intervening in a child's activities such as building a castle. Dr. Thomas Gordon, author of *Parent Effectiveness Training: The Proven Program for Raising Responsible Children* (a book I highly recommend), writes, "The parent who keeps away from the child and occupies himself with an activity of his own, permitting the child to make 'mistakes' or create his own unique design for the castle . . . —that parent is sending a non-verbal message of acceptance."[24]

"Many parents fail to realize how frequently they communicate non-acceptance to their children simply by interfering, introducing, moving in, checking up, joining in," Dr. Gordon notes.[25] When we do this, children feel like we do not trust them to figure things out, that it's not OK to make mistakes. You are better off letting children learn from their small mistakes and to handle the consequences of their actions, than having them suddenly rebel and taking all their freedom at 16 with no regard to or understanding of mistakes and consequences. Some early training in making mistakes and learning how actions have consequences might help protect them during that period.

Nonacceptance is also communicated through criticism, preaching, and ordering, he notes. So backing off of your children, and allowing them to learn from their mistakes (which also leaves you with more time for your needs) can lead to everyone being happier and better adjusted.

There is a growing body of literature that insists that micromanaging your kids' lives might actually be bad for them. This new wave of parenting refutes the smothering of children otherwise known as helicoptering, hyperparenting, alpha-parenting, or child-centered parenting. *New York Times Magazine* writer Lisa Belkin wrote a recent article about these parents. "They are saying 'no' to prenatal Beethoven appreciation classes, homework tutors in kindergarten, or moving to a town near their child's college campus so the darling can more easily have home-cooked meals."[26]

Carl Honoré coined the term "slow parenting" and is the author of *In Praise of Slow*. "Slow," he says, "does not mean doing everything at a snail's pace. It means doing everything at the right speed. That implies quality over quantity; real and meaningful human connections; being present and in the moment. The Slow creed can be applied to everything we do: work, sports, medicine, food, sex, design . . . and, of course, child rearing." "To me," he continues, "Slow Parenting is about bringing balance into the home. Children need to strive and struggle and stretch themselves but that does not mean childhood should be a race. Slow parents give their children plenty of time and space to explore the world on their own terms. They keep the family schedule under control so that everyone has enough downtime to rest, reflect and just hang out together. They accept that bending over backwards to give children the best of everything may not always be the best policy (because it denies them the much more useful life lesson of how to make the best of what they've got)."[27]

Less micromanagement allows children to make some mistakes and to learn from them. By allowing them to make mistakes, you are also showing them acceptance.

Acceptance is an important component offered by therapists to their clients. It is one of the reasons why people are often able to resolve their problems and grow by spending time with their therapists. If you want your child to open up to you and if you want to help them learn to solve their problems, then acceptance is an important ingredient.

Dr. Gordon describes the process well: "When a person is able to feel and communicate genuine acceptance of another, he possesses a capacity for being a powerful helping agent for the other. His acceptance of the other, as he is, is an important factor in fostering a relationship in which the other can grow, develop and make constructive changes, learn to solve problems, move in the direction of psychological health, become more productive and creative, and actualize his fullest potential."[28]

It is difficult for most parents, including myself, to fully grasp the concept of accepting the child even though they might be doing things that are "unacceptable." Dr. Gordon understands this concern, and says that accepting the child does not mean that the child will remain as he or she is, nor does it mean to accept all behavior. What it does achieve is to encourage them to open up and share their feelings and concerns with you.[29]

I understand acceptance as something deeper than being in relation to the behavior the child is displaying at any particular moment. I understand it as a deep sense of accepting where the child is at that point in their lives—accepting that they think and feel what they think and feel—and giving them the freedom to be their own person. Accepting includes the acknowledgment that you do not *own* this child—it therefore includes seeing yourself as a separate person from them. It means not exerting psychological control over your child, or expecting them to simply adhere to your judgments, values, and goals without questioning them.

I have come across many adults who never felt acceptance by one or more of their parents and still feel the pain of it into their adulthood. I have also come across adults who seem to have been accepted by their parents and flourish internally as a result.

I am still an amateur at applying these concepts effectively, but I have seen the positive effects of doing so and I encourage mothers to reflect on this concept and read more about it. It is an important ingredient for your children's internal peace. By accepting them, they will also learn to accept and love themselves. What better gift can you offer a child?

Her Generosity

As a first time mother, I spent the first 12 months of my son's life giving as much as I possibly could. Thus is the nature of motherhood and its capacity for unlimited generosity. My son did not even whimper without me rushing to assist him and doing whatever I could to satisfy his every possible need. I thought it was my duty as a good mother to make my son happy all the time, and I know I'm not alone. I see a lot of parents around me thinking this way.

As single mothers, we might be even more prone to doing this. In my case, for years there was no spouse or other children around taking my attention, so it was completely directed at my son.

As time passed, I slowly began to realize that it is in nobody's interest to give *too* much to children. A Single Mother in Charge knows that generosity does not mean giving too much. *Given less is often giving more*. There are several reasons for this.

Children whose every need is promptly met will end up expecting their life to unfold this way all the time. When their needs are not met perfectly and immediately, they will get more frustrated. They'll be way behind children who have learned, in some measure, that they can't get everything they want, and to have patience. By giving too much, you are creating a child who will have difficulty dealing with life's usual frustrations.

Richard Bromfield, Ph.D., and a clinical faculty member at Harvard Medical School, has been working with children and teenagers for 26 years. In his book *How to Unspoil Your Child Fast*, he pointed out that "by trying to make life too easy, by striving to bring only smiles and laughter, parents risk precisely what they fear most: children with paper-thin self-esteem who haplessly rely on outside things for stimulation, satisfaction and happiness."[30]

If your child is "spoiled," it sometimes says more about you than about your child. Try to figure out what the underlying motivation for "spoiling" your kids comes from. Is it for reasons of guilt, overcompensation, stress, your need for love, a personal need for recognition or belonging? Parents who are too permissive end up allowing the child to do anything and get everything they want. They give in to all their demands, and there is no clear limitation on unacceptable behavior. These children are not taught to have regard for how things affect other people, and they always expect to get their way. The result: children of permissive parents remain immature, tend to be impulsive, don't do well in school, and have behavior problems. Ironically, though the parents are trying hard to make them happy, these children are often unhappy, lack self-control, and do not accept responsibility for their actions.

A child who expects all their requests to be met never learns to cope with the reality of things not always going their way. And of course, this is a very important life lesson. Children get more upset about not getting what they want when they are used to getting everything. Give less, and, ironically, they might be happier.

If you are too permissive, then consider reading some books about this or enrolling in an educational program for parents.

Giving too much also applies to giving too much attention to a child. A healthy amount of "neglect" might be good for children. When we pay too much attention to our children, they lose out on the valuable skill of learning how to be alone, and even how to enjoy it. This is a life skill that can help in adulthood when times of aloneness will undoubtedly arise.

Giving too much attention probably tends to happen even more in homes where there is only one child who does not have to share the attention with other children. It's not easy, but the best way to do it is to give yourself more time and attention and try to not always deal with children's requests on demand.

The beginning of this new attitude might be strange to you and your children at first, but you will both be better off in the long run. When a child comes with some unimportant request and you are in the middle of something for yourself, don't allow yourself to be interrupted. There are many of us who do not even get to take a three-minute shower in peace without someone asking for something.

So as a start, refuse to answer anything while you are in the shower. The same goes for unimportant discussions after bedtime.

It's hard for single mothers to do these things, I know—especially if we have not kicked out the "single-mother guilt" we discussed in Section 2. But getting into these kinds of little good habits one by one will lead to a better balance between the attention you give your children and the attention you give yourself. This will make you into a better mother—which is good for them and good for you.

Her Authenticity

When we become parents, we often forget that we are human. We think we have to behave in ways that "parents" should and forget that we are humans with real feelings. For a healthy interaction between mother and child, the mother should be *herself* and be *authentic*. This means not faking some "parental role" that you are supposed to have, but instead being and showing your child that you are a real human being, with feelings, disappointments, frustrations, and needs. This will create a more genuine relationship with your children because they will see you as a "real" person.[31]

Try being authentic with your children. Accept yourself, then, *be* yourself—as you are. Honesty and openness are necessary ingredients to a healthy personal relationship. For example, pretending you don't mind something when in fact you do is not authentic and real. If you pretend something doesn't bother you when it does, your child is getting mixed messages because they can still see your facial expression and sense your inner tension. You are better off being authentic and expressing your real feelings when the moment comes. Your child will see you as an open and honest person rather than a fake.

Dr. Thomas Gordon, author of *Parent Effectiveness Training*, teaches that authentic does not mean simply putting down the child whenever you feel like it. Authentic means to try to see what *you are feeling* and communicating this to the child.

The first step is to become aware of your needs. Kids have needs, but so do you. Allowing your children to take over the house and ignore *your* needs is in nobody's interest. Dr. Gordon points out that "when parents permit this to happen, their children move through life as if it is a one way street for the continuous gratification of their own needs. Parents of such children usually become embittered, and feel strong resentment toward their 'ungrateful' 'selfish' kids."[32]

So the first step is to get to know what your needs are. Do you need quiet to work or relax? Do you need space to finish the cooking? Do you need a moment to finish your phone conversation? Realize that your needs matter! When something happens, communicate it to your child, and Dr. Gordon recommends doing it with authentic language about what you need or feel.

For example, telling your child "I can't concentrate and finish my work when there is so much noise," or "I felt worried sick about you when you didn't call from the mall" is more authentic and communicates your needs. Using accusing language or orders such as "Stop it!" or "How could you forget to call? You're so irresponsible!" does not communicate your needs and feelings effectively, nor explain what effect the child's behavior has on you.

So instead of saying "Can't you just be quiet for a minute when I'm on the phone," Dr. Gordon suggests speaking in "I" messages. For example, you can say "When you speak to me when I'm on the phone, I can't hear what the other person is saying and I get so distracted." You are teaching them what the impact of their actions are (which children often do not realize!).

By doing this, you are being authentic by expressing your needs and how you feel. And by not suggesting a solution, and simply expressing the effect it had on you, you are inviting the child to figure out how to solve this problem for the future. As Dr. Gordon says, "I-Messages help a child learn how to assume responsibility for her own behavior. An I-Message tells a child that you are leaving the responsibility with her, trusting her to respect your needs, giving her a chance to start behaving constructively."[33] You are also teaching self-discipline and creating a conscience.

I recommend that every parent consider reading this book to see whether they can learn how to express their needs in a healthy way to their children.

Sally (not her real name), a single mom of three boys, has seen the benefits of authenticity. She said: "I just feel like I was forced to explain a lot of things most kids don't get explained to them. And I have this policy of almost bold-faced honesty. So I tell 'em like it is 99 percent of the time. And we have a deeper understanding of each other—my flaws as well as my attributes."

When you accept yourself and your child, and act authentically, you are on your way to developing an honest relationship with your child. When something interferes with your needs, express your feelings, whether it was feeling hurt or frustrated or whatever. Let them know you are a real person, and they will often choose to modify their behavior so that it doesn't negatively affect you. This kindness, empathy, acceptance, and adapting to each other's needs will help build an authentic and deeper relationship—not to mention teaching your kids to consider other people's needs and to be responsible for their actions!

Once your children learn how their behavior affects others, they will start to self-regulate, and the positive effects of this will spiral. It will lead to even more positive reinforcement from extended family, teachers, and others. They will be more liked by others, and this is generally good for their self-esteem. It's a win-win situation.

Her Leadership

Do you continuously do things for your kids that they can do for themselves? Do you think that they will think you love them more if you make their beds every day or slave around? Do you think it is a sign of good mothering to always pick up their toys? A Single Mother in Charge entrusts her children to do what they are capable of doing on their own. She knows how to delegate.

From this moment on, try not to do things that don't fall under your responsibilities. Remember that the goal is to raise adults who are responsible, self-sufficient, and independent. Doing things for them that they can do for themselves is counterproductive. Older children can make their own breakfasts (and perhaps occasional suppers). Older children can take care of their own rooms and laundry. Perhaps they can make dinner for the family one night a week (including setting the table and doing the dishes). They will also feel good about participating in and accomplishing making a nice dinner. This will also free up some time for you, which I'm sure you need and deserve!

Single-mother families tend to be more interdependent and more inclined to work together. Single moms need the cooperation of their children, and I think this is a good thing for children. Young people like to feel needed and to feel that their contributions are valuable. It makes them feel important and like they belong to a team.

Letting natural consequences occur is also a useful learning experience to teach responsibility. Some situations lend themselves well to natural consequences. If your child forgets to take something they need to the pool, they will learn from that experience. There is no need to get upset or to preach in those situations. The child will learn from their own experience.

Let the child learn from the problems they encounter in their daily lives. Teaching children to find their own solutions to their problems and how to be responsible is an amazing gift for a child. If you jump in every time they have a problem, this does not "help" them. It deprives them from learning how to deal with difficulty, find solutions, and increase their confidence in their own abilities to cope with life.

My son came home one day and told me about a child in school who was bothering him every day. I didn't get upset, call the other mother or the principal, offer him advice, preach or judge. I simply listened to him. Once he told me everything, I said to him, "You seem to be handling the situation on your own, trying different tactics to deal with him." I asked if he needed my help. He said no. He told me a bit more over the next few days. He discussed different tactics he was trying. Eventually, it was resolved without my interference.

When I let my son struggle with something that I could solve for him in one second, he benefits by feeling good about being able to achieve things and feeling more independent. He learns that he is capable of handling a lot of situations. I am hoping that he is acquiring the skills necessary to handle regular daily problems by himself.

Sometimes the best way to help is to simply listen, what Dr. Gordon calls "active listening," without judgment or advice, similar to what therapists do. The listening has to be done with empathy. He suggests that children should own their problems and find their own solutions. This allows the child to reflect **on their own** and solve their own problems. It also makes the child feel accepted. And it enables the child to express themselves and eventually find their own solutions without having been judged, directed, criticized, preached to, warned, blamed, or even sympathized with.[34] Simple active listening can go a long way in many situations. This sort of listening also opens up all the lines of communication.

We all say we want better communication with our children, but you cannot have it simply by dictating, judging, and preaching. Good communication necessarily entails validating and seeing your child as their own person and accepting how they are feeling, irrespective of whether you think they *should* feel it. I highly recommend Dr. Gordon's book to help you delve deeper into these theories and test them out on your child. I am confident that learning these skills will allow your communication with your children to reach another level. This will naturally solve a host of other problems you might be experiencing due to lack of good communication.

When we help our children too much (which I admit I am still working on), the child will always turn to you for help in times of need. Now that might sound like a good thing, but in fact, it's important for children to learn how to solve their own problems. If you solve everything for your child, they do not learn how to think of solutions. Of course, this is all about the size of the problem. Children should start to learn how to solve small problems appropriate for their age while feeling they can come to you for help and support for bigger problems.

Marano writes in *A Nation of Wimps* of David Anderegg, a child psychologist in Lenox, Massachusetts, and professor of psychology at Bennington College. He says that "anxious parents are hyperattentive to their kids, reactive to every blip of their child's day, eager to solve every problem for their child—and believe that's good parenting."[35]

"I wish my parents had some hobby other than me," one young patient told Anderegg. "If you have an infant and the baby has gas, burping the baby is being a good parent. But when you have a 10-year-old who has metaphoric gas, you don't have to burp him. You have to let him sit with it, try to figure out what to do about it. He then learns to tolerate moderate amounts of difficulty, and it's not the end of the world."[36]

Harvard psychologist Jerome Kagan has conducted numerous studies on children and their temperaments. His studies have shown unequivocally that "what creates anxious children is parents hovering and protecting them from stressful experiences."[37]

A Single Mother in Charge, while keeping a watchful eye, lets her cubs learn to cope with life.

Her Attitude

Once you have mastered having a more positive attitude yourself, it's time to see how you can improve your children's explanatory style. We can literally inject optimism into our children!

For example, if they come home from school saying "I'm such a bad student," try to discuss this with them. Try to show teach them how not to "enlarge" or dramatize situations by equating difficulty with one subject at school into being a bad student overall. Make sure your own explanatory style is also consistent with this. Teach them how not to turn setbacks into catastrophes. Being more optimistic will enable them to better bounce back from negative experiences.

A positive attitude and optimistic explanatory style early in life can affect their health and well-being later in life. It is pure preventative medicine for children. Martin Seligman, author of *The Optimistic Child*, has been running programs to teach these skills to children, aimed at safeguarding them from depression as adults.

It will be easier for you to teach your child optimism and how to increase their happiness if you have done the job first on yourself. Happiness is contagious, so the more you work on yourself, the more you can pass on to your children. They will use you as an example. In fact, a huge study published in December 2008 in the *British Medical Journal* documented findings on the contagious nature of happiness. American scientists followed 4,700 people for more than 20 years and found that happy people boost the chances that their friends, neighbors, siblings, and family will be happy. Their happiness can even ripple through people they don't know.

And the effects of one person's happiness on another can last for up to a year.[38]

"Happiness is like a stampede," according to Harvard professor Nicholas Christakis. "Whether you're happy or not depends not just on your own actions and behaviors and thoughts, but on those of people you don't even know."[39]

We have all experienced this. Our bad attitude can affect our children. But the good news is that our good attitude will too! So the first step to teaching your children to be positive is to first adopt the approach yourself. Start with one day. Just commit to one full day of having a positive attitude and see what effect it has on your children.

If you need any more reasons to do so, how about for your children's health? A multitude of research has linked a positive attitude to better health. Do it together! The results will be magnificent!

Her Encouragement

A Single Mother in Charge is very attentive to her children's level of self-esteem. She knows that raising self-esteem in a child is not achieved through telling them they're great or saying "good job" every five minutes. I used to do this a lot but now realize that giving too much praise to a child can have the opposite effect. Ironically, it can lead to being less able to cope with life's inevitable setbacks.

I think the only thing that happens when we praise too much is that the child no longer takes the praise seriously. Or conversely, they are always seeking praise for their efforts.

It's critical to realize that parental praise is *not* the source of a child's self-esteem. Nor is it the source of an adult's self-esteem, for that matter. "It's so common now for parents to tell children that they're special," says Jean Twenge, an associate professor of psychology at San Diego State University and author of *Generation Me*.[40] That fosters narcissism, she says, not self-esteem.

Similarly, there is a danger of linking self-esteem to the material things kids own. Materialism is a coping strategy for low self-worth. A new study in the *Journal of Consumer Research* by Lan Nguyen Chaplin from the University of Illinois at Urbana-Champaign and Deborah Roedder John of the University of Minnesota found that there may be an actual causal relationship between materialism and low self-esteem in teenagers.[41] Low self-esteem may cause an increase in materialism, and materialism may create low self-esteem. As self-esteem increases, you can expect to see a drop in materialism. Instead of teaching kids to develop self-esteem by the things they *own*, you are better off trying to help them develop it by their character, their efforts, or other ways. People often shop because there is something missing in their lives. But you are better off trying to fill what's missing than living the illusion that the temporary pleasure of shopping will fill that void.

In my experience, self-esteem in children is a by-product of three important elements. The first is a parenting style that includes acceptance, love, and appropriate limits, as discussed earlier.

The second is for a child to feel important, needed, and worthy. This is achieved through encouraging the child to participate and be valuable. It can be at home with chores, helping to teach younger kids in karate class, participating in a charitable or school event, or some other method where a child feels helpful, valuable, and needed. I remember my son going out for Halloween and knocking on doors for candy one year and how much fun that was for him. Several days later, he participated in a food drive for the local food depot and went door-to-door as a Boy Scout collecting canned goods for the poor. I can assure you he enjoyed and got a lot more out of getting those cans for the poor than getting candy for himself. Kids love to feel useful and needed!

Finally, self-esteem in your children is built when they *try things and make progress* (whether or not the ultimate goal is achieved every time). This means that the child will feel good about themselves when they try things and progress or learn.

Let's take two typical scenarios.

Child 1 is stacking blocks and they fall. The child is discouraged and doesn't want to build anymore. If you are used to always "praising," you say "good job" and that's where the experience ends.

Child 2 is stacking blocks and they fall. The child gets upset. You encourage the child to keep trying and praise them for their efforts. The child keeps trying and is finally able to build higher and higher.

Which do you think builds self-esteem? It seems obvious that the scenario that includes challenges, failures, and progress is the way to go. The second child has greater self-confidence from knowing that they have an ability to learn and master tasks.

Nathaniel Branden, author of the *Art of Living Consciously*, writes that "the root of our self-esteem is not our achievements per se but those internally generated practices that make it possible for us to achieve. How much we will achieve in the world is not fully in our control. An economic depression can temporarily put us out of work. A depression cannot take away the resourcefulness that will allow us sooner or later to find another or go into business for ourselves. 'Resourcefulness' is not an achievement in the world (although it may result in that); it is an action in consciousness—and it is here that self-esteem is generated."[42]

Thus it is an error to measure personal worth by our external achievements. Rather, he defines self-esteem as "the disposition to experience oneself as being competent to cope with the basic challenges of life and of being worthy of happiness. It is confidence in the efficacy of our mind, in our ability to think. By extension, it is confidence in our ability to learn, make appropriate choices and decisions, and respond effectively to change. It is also the experience that success, achievement, fulfillment—happiness—are right and natural for us. The survival-value of such confidence is obvious; so is the danger when it is missing."[43]

So one key element to building children's self-esteem is to put appropriate challenges in front of them, and if it looks like they're going to fail, let them! When they finally do progress or succeed, it is not your praise that makes them feel good about themselves, but their own feeling of being proud of themselves. Even if they "fail" they will feel proud of themselves for not being afraid to try things.

You can praise efforts, which they now deserve, without focusing just on their success. Most people are not geniuses, and numerous studies have found that intelligence accounts for only a fraction of success. What seems to make a significant difference is persistence and tenacity, also known as "grit." Teaching persistence is invaluable to a child's future.

For example, I often take my son on hikes up mountains. There is one in particular that we hike up and that he has hiked since he was four. It takes over an hour to get up, going uphill, climbing some rocks along the way, and dealing with the occasional scraped knees. Of course, the first time took constant encouragement, but I truly believed he could make it up to the summit. He did and he was proud of himself for doing so. Since then I have gone about half a dozen times with other kids and my son. My son feels prouder of himself every time because he feels he's gone up more times than they have and finds it easier. He also attacks any climbing challenge with no hesitation as a result, and ends up achieving other things as well. It just spirals from there. He's often told people, "I'm a really good climber." It's not because I told him he is. It's because he's climbed and achieved. When he was seven, I upped the challenge and went up a mountain that was 2,871 feet with my uncle and his seven- and nine-year-old children. It took us over three hours, but when we were up

ARE YOUR KIDS SMART OR HARD-WORKING?

Research indicates that praising kids for their innate ability or intelligence ("you must be smart") as opposed to their efforts ("you must have worked hard"), might have some undesired impact on children's overall achievement. Columbia University researchers Claudia Mueller and Carol Dweck (author of *Mindset*) found that children who were praised for their intelligence as opposed to their efforts became overly focused on performance as opposed to learning opportunities. Following a failure, these same children persisted less, enjoyed the tasks less, and attributed their failure to a lack of ability (which they believed is a fixed trait and could not change). "Praising children for intelligence makes them fear difficulty because they begin to equate failure with stupidity." "The kind of praise that all of society thinks is wonderful is the kind of praise that makes kids very vulnerable," says Dweck, "Parents need to focus on what children put into a task, rather than making implications about the worth of the child."

Source: "Praise for Intelligence Can Undermine Children's Motivation and Performance," *Journal of Personality and Social Psychology*, 1998, Vol 75, No. 1, 33–52. https://www.stanford.edu/dept/psychology/cgi-bin/drupalm/system/files/Intelligence%20Praise%20Can%20Undermine%20Motivation%20and%20Performance.pdf. Last accessed March 18, 2010; http://www.psychologytoday.com/articles/199709/praising-your-child. Last accessed March 18, 2010.

in the clouds, exhausted after three hours. Boy, were the kids proud of themselves. I was even proud of myself!! These kinds of experiences are unforgettable for kids.

You can put your children in activities that encourage this kind of learning. I chose karate for my son. He started at four and it took him a whole year to achieve the next level, a yellow belt. Believe me, the look on his face whenever he gets a belt is irreplaceable because he earns them all by himself.

Another challenge we did together is walk a half marathon (which took us over four hours to complete). But he has that medal, which he earned all by himself with his sore feet. He now doesn't see a 10-minute walk as such a big deal.

Challenge your children with something appropriate for their age and skill. Praise their efforts, celebrating not only the destination but also the journey. Or, as recommended by Jim Taylor, Ph.D., "go out on a limb and don't say anything at all to your children. As I just mentioned, kids know when they do well. By letting them come to this realization on their own, they learn to reinforce themselves and they don't become praise junkies dependent on you for how they feel about their efforts and accomplishments."[44]

One thing to remember is that the challenges should be just slightly harder than their current level, just slightly outside their comfort zone, and then should be increased incrementally. They should not be extreme or unachievable, which would then defeat the purpose if failure is always inevitable. Ideas don't have to be complicated. It can be as simple as letting them cross streets alone, trying a kayak alone, letting them do their own laundry, letting them try to help with tools that are new to them, and letting them figure out how to solve day-to-day problems that are a bit challenging to them. This will give them confidence in their ability to think, learn, and cope with challenges in life.

And by accepting them and letting them make some mistakes through this process, you have touched on some very important ingredients of self-esteem.

Her Family Time

Television distracts us from the essence of life. Yet the average American home has more TVs than people.[45] And the average teenager watches an unbelievable average of 3 hours and 20 minutes of TV a day![46]

We have all used the TV, computers, and video games as "electronic babysitters," but the effects of too much of these are going to be more trouble in the long run. TV not only encourages violence and materialism, but also steals time away from an opportunity to connect, reflect, cry, grow, play, rest, or simply be aware of being alive. In babies, recent studies show that time spent watching TV inhibits their social, cognitive, and language development. TV can slow down babies' likelihood of acquiring new vocabulary and playing and interacting with others.[47] Because watching TV hampers rich interaction, no matter what's playing, and even if the parents interact while watching TV together, the effect was a drop in vocalizations.[48] And evidence is mounting about the effect of baby DVD's on language development as well. Frederick Zimmerman, a University of Washington professor of health services says regarding a 2007 study he co-authored, "there is no clear evidence of a benefit coming from baby DVDs and videos and there is some suggestion of harm."[49]

Teaching your children how to keep themselves busy and to entertain themselves might be difficult at first, especially if the TV, video games, and computer have become a real habit, but it is something that can be developed.

Many parents do not allow their children to be bored and schedule every moment of a child's life. "Parents worry about kids' boredom, so they schedule their lives to keep them busy," say Alvin Rosenfeld, a child psychiatrist and Nicole Wise, authors of *The Over-Scheduled Child*.[50] But boredom is a great thing!! Experts say that these empty hours can teach children how to create their own happiness. They will find ways to amuse themselves, even if it's just daydreaming! Boredom helps fuel creativity.

Richard Louv, senior editor of the Washington, D.C.-based group Connect for Kids, and author of *Last Child in the Woods*, has said that "children need adults in their lives who understand the relationship between boredom and creativity—and are willing to set the stage so that kids can create the play."[51] So encourage unstructured play by turning off the TV and by making sure your child has time that is not spent in structured activities.

There's another benefit to turning off the TV, says James Steyer, a Stanford University law professor and author of *The Other Parent: The Inside Story of the Media's Effect on Our Children*. "If another adult spent five or six hours a day with your kids, regularly exposing them to sex, violence and rampantly commercial values, you would probably forbid that person to have further contact with them," Steyer says. "Yet most of us passively allow the media to expose our kids routinely to these same behaviors . . . and do virtually nothing about it."[52] A Single Mother in Charge offers her kids the gift of empty hours, and is wise enough to allow her children to develop during that time.

When she can, the Single Mother in Charge encourages physical activity for the physical and mental well-being of her children. John Ratey, a Harvard clinical associate professor of psychiatry, and author of *Spark: The Revolutionary New Science of Exercise and the Brain*, argues that exercise is good not only for physical health, but also for getting better grades. He writes, "Exercise stimulates our gray matter to produce Miracle-Gro for the brain. Dopamine, serotonin, norepinephrine—all of these are elevated after exercise. So having a workout will help focus, calming down, and impulsivity—it's like taking a little bit of Prozac and a little bit of Ritalin."[53]

If you don't have the time or money to send your children to activities, then send them outside, if they are old enough, to dribble a basketball. If they're too young, then a walk to the park will get them moving and busy.

Ideally, get your kids to spend more time outdoors. Andrea Faber Taylor and Frances Kuo, researchers at the Human Environment Research Laboratory at the University of Illinois at Urbana-Champaign, have documented the positive effects of "green" settings on ADHD patients. By simply incorporating nature in their activities, as opposed to indoor playgrounds and human-made recreation areas, researchers have found a dramatic reduction in symptoms.[54] The benefits of "green time" for all of us is that: it has no side effects, it's nonstigmatizing, and it's free!

To increase "green time," try finding a different route for kids to get to school, encourage kids to do homework outside or near a window, and of course, engage in outdoor activities instead of dragging kids to the mall or keeping them "protected" inside. They need nature. Otherwise, we might be facing a wide range of behavioral problems caused by, what Richard Louv calls, "nature-deficit disorder."[55]

Her Connection with Her Kids

In Section 4, we discussed the importance of having relationships and happiness. This applies to your children as well. They need relationships and this begins with you! You are the primary relationship in your child's life, and it's a very important one to cultivate.

Most of us want to have a harmonious child-parent relationship, but unfortunately many parents do not have this with their children. Most children need to feel unconditional love and acceptance, and to know that they are heard, respected, and valued. But unfortunately, sometimes the relationship is so broken down, the parents no longer even "like" their kids and just want to get away from them.

I won't start by telling you to have more "quality time" together. (I'm not a big fan of this old cliché.) I have observed many parents making great efforts to take their children to circuses, resorts, and other activities, and in spite of all this fun, there doesn't seem to be a strong connection between the child and the parent. I have also seen other families in which the child and the parent seem very connected, even when doing the basics. It shows in their eyes, not in their activities.

Many people think the solution is to deal with their children's behavior. They think the solution lies in becoming less permissive or stricter with their children's behavior and for some, this might be the case. But I'm not sure this is the solution to "connection issues" with your child. I think the real solutions are deeper. I doubt you can solve this problem with some new parenting book about discipline—a deeper analysis of the situation is needed.

To begin, I invite you to question what level of connection you feel with your children and how they feel with you. How do you rate your relationship right now? Be honest with yourself and accept this as the starting point, even if it is not very good. And now, regardless of where you stand or what your current level of connection, the next question you should ask is: Where do I go from here? How can I improve our relationship?

In my experience, the subtle elements required to improve a relationship are found all over the pages of this book. For example, letting go of your negative emotions, such as anger and guilt, and reducing anxiety will affect your relationship with your kids. Filling your cup by adopting a positive attitude to life, exercising, improving your self-esteem and self-respect, being aware of your feelings, simplifying your life, and being in nature will also contribute. Similarly, accepting and understanding your children, your role, yourself, and your instincts will help. As will all the other strategies discussed, like being authentic and giving the child room to grow. There is no parenting style that will work if these underlying ingredients are missing. *So working on those strategies will lead to improving all your relations, including those with your children.*

But let me add some final few pointers to help you build connection and a loving bond with your children. As you will see, sometimes it's the small things that count:

Eye contact: An old Yiddish proverb says, "The eyes are the mirror of the soul," showing our innermost thoughts. If you pay attention, you might realize you are often looking at the dishes, laundry, stove, fridge, or lunchbox while talking to your child. I know we are all busy, but we can take some time to read the eyes of our children and to listen to them while looking at them. It will send the message, that you are interested in what they are speaking about. It will also allow you to understand them better by reading their body language. And your body language matters too. A sincere smile, a pat on the head, and other friendly gestures—these unspoken cues can often transmit *much more* than words.

Connect physically: When you first see your children in the morning, say "good morning." When you pick them up from school, greet them warmly, preferably with a hug. I think this physical contact is particularly important for children between the ages of 4 and 15. Before 4, many parents are quite physical with their children because of their basic needs of being carried or because parents tend to be more demonstrative with small children. But who do your children touch after that? Unless they are physically demonstrative with their friends, or eventually girlfriends and boyfriends, there might be long periods of time, even years, where they are getting *no physical affection at all with anyone* during this age range. Dr. Tiffany Field discusses how vital touch is in her book *Touch*. She is also the founder of Touch Research Institute at the University of Miami School of Medicine in 1992, the first center in the world devoted solely to the study of touch and its application in science and medicine.[56] We cannot underestimate the power of touch. We prepare their lunches, drive them around, try to meet their constant needs, which is all a sign of love, but physical contact helps a child feel secure and loved. If it feels weird to restart this with a 10-year-old you haven't hugged in a long time, start with pats on the head, then arms around shoulders, and go from there.

Participate with them: We often bring kids to activities, friends' houses, or other places of their choice, and let them go at it alone. What a child sometimes needs, however, is for you to participate in the activity with them. I know your time as a single mother is limited, but once in a while allocate 15 minutes to a child and ask them what they want to do with you. Participate in their activity whatever it is, whether playing a video game or climbing something.

Spend time with each child individually: Try to spend even a few moments with one child without the other around. They need time with you alone, even if it's a few minutes before bed.

Actions speak louder than words: How many of us have experienced being treated badly one day by someone and then being told nice things by the same person the next day. Think back to previous relationships and make a list of what was *said* to you and what was actually *done*. When we size people up based on their *actions*, don't we have a much clearer understanding of who that person is? With our children, we can follow the same principle and realize the limitations of words and the importance of actions. If you love someone, you *treat them* a certain way. Words are not enough. Although it might be nice for us or our children to hear the words "I love you," actions matter most!

Do not lie to your children, ever: Some of you might justify lying to your children because of their age or to protect them. But I would argue that lying to children at any age is highly detrimental to the relationship. Trust is crucial to maintain connection with your child. Does that mean that you need to expose every detail you experience or are asked about by your children? Absolutely not! If your child asks what you were telling the person on the phone, you need not divulge this. You can simply say "These are adult matters" or "It's nothing you need to worry about." This is better than lying and pretending something else occurred or that you were talking to someone else. If your child asks why you and your ex-husband divorced, you can choose what you want to say and need not divulge all the personal details to a young child.

When a parent lies to a child, they think the child doesn't realize it, but if you look in their eyes, you can see the doubt they feel in their parents. This hurts the trust relationship between a parent and child as much as using sarcasm, ridicule, insults, and similar communication breaches.

Eat together: Researchers have found that eating together was the single strongest predictor of better test scores and fewer behavioral problems. And research from the Center on Addiction and Substance Abuse (CASA) at Columbia University has "consistently found that children who have frequent family dinners are less likely to use marijuana, tobacco and drink alcohol."[57] With work, activities, homework, and housework, it might seem inconvenient to sit and eat together every night but the rewards far outweigh the effort. Mealtime is an opportunity to communicate and connect with your child. Eating together is a foundation for a better relationship. It's hard to have full conversations while taking out the garbage or folding laundry. You find out about each other's days, problems, etc., and give some attention to your children while eating together. It's also a perfect opportunity to teach basic social graces, like good table manners and the art of conversation, so essential later in life. And getting different children doing tasks like setting the table, cleaning up, and serving is a cooperative activity that teaches children how to participate with others.

Act like a family: I know many single mothers have a hard time using the word *family* when speaking about themselves with their children. But try it sometime, and use it long enough—you'll be amazed at how natural it feels. Kids like to be part of a family, whether it's two people or more. Give yourself and your kids the right to use this label.

Make every child feel needed and included: Sometimes it's the little things that make the child feel included, which you can do even when you don't have much time or are busy. For example, you can invite your child to do their homework at the kitchen table while you are cooking. Or invite your older child to come along for grocery shopping, even if you think they will say no. They will still feel good about being asked to come along. Extra smiles, pats on the head, or hugs for no reason also go a long way toward achieving this goal.

I consciously try to make sure my son feels needed ... because he is.

Her Flexibility

I remember telling my kung-fu teacher one day about how I was experiencing some problems and how happy I was to be able to come to class to keep me strong. His answer: "It's good to be strong, but it's also important to remain supple."

I realize that just as flexibility is necessary in the practice of kung-fu, it is necessary in life as well. Strength coupled with flexibility allows you to make better decisions about your life.

I do not pretend to be an expert on anything I have written in this book. During the process of writing this book, my own thoughts on so many of these topics were continuously evolving. I also expect that after it is published, my thoughts might continue to evolve, and I invite that growth. I know my perspectives might change with time.

Having this flexibility, this openness to change, allows us to adapt to our ever-changing needs and those of our children. And allows us to adapt to the ever-changing life circumstances we face.

It allows us to adopt new strategies with our children when needed, or when previous ones are no longer working. It allows us to explore new ways of living when our old ways don't make us happy. It allows us to be open to new ideas that are good for us instead of being stuck in our same old ways. I am a student and will forever be a student.

Having flexibility coupled with strength allows us to change when we believe it's time to do something different. Flexibility takes courage. Many people are stuck in one way of living or thinking because change, to them, means that they have to admit they were previously wrong. I don't see it that way. Rather, we are all evolving and learning and doing what we think is best at each point of our lives. It's not about right or wrong, but rather about learning and growing.

I do not know what the future holds. But I have certainly learned a lot, cried a lot, and tried hard. I do hope that something good will come from my efforts, but I will accept any reality and truth and go from there.

Her Parenting Goals

We have now arrived at the last chapter. What a journey it has been to grow and learn through this process. Yet for the five years I have been writing this book, I have always had a feeling that things were incomplete. There was something missing and I couldn't put my finger on it. Several months before my manuscript was due I finally got a hint of what was missing.

On the day it came to me, I was sitting with my girlfriend, talking about some small incident that happened with my son that day. It was a minor incident and my friend just told me not to worry since he seemed to be a super kid headed toward being very successful in life. And this is where I realized that I had not been clear in my goal when raising my child. For years I had been learning and gathering many different ingredients on how to be happier and how to raise a happier child (which led to all the strategies in this book). But my goal was not clear enough, and this is why I always felt there was something missing. I wasn't clear on what my motivation was for practicing all the strategies I had learned. I *thought* it was so I could be happier and raise a happier child. I *thought* it was so we would have a good relationship. Yet even though I felt relatively well balanced and happy most of the time, and that my son was as well, and that our relationship was better than ever, I still felt like something was incomplete. Something was still missing.

Until this moment, I hadn't realized the deeper goal and meaning behind this endeavor. But when my friend mentioned that my son would likely be successful, these words came out of my mouth:

"My goal is not to raise a 'successful' adult, a 'doctor' or a 'lawyer,'" I told her. "These are the kinds of things he can decide for himself. It's not my job to guide my son on how to be 'successful' in that sense. I would not be happy if he became a billionaire who treated people badly. I would not be proud of that!"

This is when I realized my true goal. I was trying to improve myself first and trying to raise a decent human being, a *mentsh*. This goal was meaningful for me, and deeper than being "happy." I believe that we are born into the world to improve it. To use our strength, intelligence, tools, or whatever we have to improve the world around us. Or at least, not to harm it. This is what I am still learning about myself at a deeper level. And this is what I hope to teach my son, and for him to teach his children. Albert Einstein said, "Try to become not a man of success, but try rather to become a man of value."[58]

I then realized that the essence of many of the strategies in this book were *actually* for just that—for us to become *better*, not just happier, people. Some of the ingredients for becoming a better person were all over the pages of this book without my consciously intending it: To do good in our world, we do need to first empty our cup of anger, guilt, fear, and helplessness. To improve our world, we need courage, self-esteem, and an optimistic view of the possibilities of the world. We need self-respect, self-esteem, etc.

I remember my son's karate teacher talking to the class about getting a black belt. He said that many people think that getting a black belt is the ultimate goal. But in fact it is just the beginning! He said many senseis (teachers) simply regard getting a black belt as having become a "teachable student." I realized that getting myself well, and helping my son be balanced and happy, allowed me to have a better relationship with him. And now this is the beginning . . . It is *only now that I can be a better teacher* and he *a teachable student*. I can now try to teach him whatever values I've acquired so far (and so much believe in) to become a *mentsh*.

Leo Rosten writes about the Yiddish word *mentsh*:

To be a *mentsh* has nothing to do with success, wealth, or status. A judge can be a *zhlob*, a millionaire can be a *mamzer*, a professor can be a *shlemiel*, a doctor a klutz, a lawyer a *bulvon*. The key to being 'a real mentsh' is nothing less than character: rectitude, dignity, a sense of what is right, responsible, decorous. Many a poor person, many an ignorant person, is a *mentsh*.[59]

And when the mother and the child are able to offer something of value to the world, whether it's small gestures or big actions, whether it's for family or for strangers, they will both feel valuable because they *are* in fact valuable to others. This will lead to a true sense of self-esteem and self-worth. This is even deeper than "happiness"—it's a recipe for being at peace with who you are in this world.

As Leo Rosten said, "I cannot believe that the purpose of life is to be happy. I think the purpose of life is to be useful, to be responsible, to be compassionate. It is, above all, to matter, to count, to stand for something, to have made some difference that you lived at all."[60]

But I am but one mother . . . together we can change the world.

SECTION 6

In the Words of Single Mothers

I spent time surfing blogs, posts, and message boards online in search of comments from other single mothers about the bright side of being a single mother.[1]

They inspired me to write this book. The similarities in the experiences of so many single mothers reminded me that I was not the only one who had lived through difficulties. Nor was I the only one who was trying so hard to be optimistic, authentic and strong despite the challenges for the sake of my child.

Here are some of my favorites from my findings.* I hope they encourage you and help you to remember that **you are not alone**!

ON FEAR

- I can laugh when dinner burns instead of being afraid.
- Never have to worry about him beating me or abusing me emotionally, spiritually, mentally, psychologically.
- Not having to deal with baseless accusations of being unfaithful. Oh yeah . . . because every married woman who's 39 weeks pregnant wants to try to sexually satisfy more than one man.
- I don't have to deal with crazy mood swings, and constantly be the cheerleader, bread winner, house cleaner, cook, shopper,

---

*I removed the typographical errors so common in the message boards where these comments were posted, to make the passages clear and easier to read for those who were not part of the activity at the time.

and then be blamed when things go wrong or that I didn't quit my job to "support" him in his "effort" to start his business (which wasn't making any money).

- No tiptoeing around the ex and his "issues" (couldn't have any noise in the house, no candles or incense because of his "allergies").

- No tiptoeing around at noon as to not wake a still sleeping adult.

- We can go to Target at 9:00 p.m. at night with no one freaking out on us (ex wouldn't let us leave the house after dark unless he was along for the ride).

- Never, ever being afraid in my own home ... Never having to wonder when the next blow-up is going to occur ... Knowing that my precious blessings are thriving in a love-filled, safe, happy, healthy home!

- No one around to cheat on me.

- Not always tensely listening for someone else stomping around the house.

- I don't have to stop normal life to prepare for the 5 p.m. arrival of Him.

- Our home is a safe place now. No verbal abuse. No emotional abuse.

- I love the fact that there is no point in the day in which I tense up b/c someone's going to walk thru the door and bring the whole house's vibe down.

- I love not feeling the fear quite so much. The fear of violence, fear of not being good enough, fear of escalating arguments started by him, fear of being a failure and being told what a failure I am, fear of constant ridicule.

- I don't have to be with a man from "need" or fear—I know I can do it on my own—the man in my life is there because he makes it better, not because I can't make it by myself.

- I don't have to walk on egg shells anymore. I get to say what I want when I want and I can tell my ex exactly what's on my mind.

- I got back my: pride, self-esteem, joy, independence, individuality, TIME, money (when I start to make some again), and peace of mind (he did something every day that caused me to worry every day "who or what or where will he do, lose, hurt, steal, or end up?????").

- I am happy to say I haven't cried myself to sleep since I left him!!!!

ON GUILT

- I never feel guilty for not wanting to have sex.
- I don't have to feel guilty about wanting sex.
- I also love "nobody makes me feel guilty about spending time with my children," so simple yet so articulate and true.
- My son once told me that although he was sometimes sad he didn't have a dad, he was really happy he didn't have a mean, horrible dad (this was when he was about seven). And that about sums it up for me, and allowed a lot of the guilt to wash away.
- The realization just hit me out of the blue, and it was almost like a revelation. I can take care of myself without feeling guilty. This is great! No more asking, no more explaining. My thoughts, choices, and feelings are valid.

ON THE END OF CONFLICT IN THE HOME

- No adults yell at me in my own home.
- No one to fight with.
- No one who lies to me.
- No adult pouting (plenty from the kid, though ;-).
- I don't have to deal with an hour of grumpy verbal abuse every morning, make his breakfast, and then hear "sorry about that . . . I love you" after he gets his coffee and a smoke!
- I am not worried that I'm being cheated on. Unless my 3-year-old is seeing another mama on the side, which would explain why she came home from daycare with different socks on yesterday.
- I don't have to worry about what time he is coming home from work or IF he is coming home from work.
- I don't have to explain to everyone why my husband didn't come with me to an event.
- I know that one loving parent is better than two who hate one another.
- My children have a happy dad who enjoys his time with them, instead of an angry dad who is perpetually burnt-out and either ignoring them or yelling at them.

- I love the peaceful aura my kids have now, instead of the nervous habits they had before.
- I loved giving my kids a happy home, the kind they always deserved, but sadly had too little of.
- I look at how amazingly smart, happy, and passionate my daughter is and think how wonderful our lives are together. I imagine the horror that was our life that I saved her from and know that leaving was the best thing I could have ever done for us.
- Everyone is respected 100 percent of the time.
- When I go home I know what to expect. PEACE.
- ......PEACE, PEACE, and more PEACE. Oh I can't tell you how good it feels.
- Man, it feels so good to live as a human.

ON PARENTING

- ... everyone who knows us thinks that *I* am doing a great job raising my sons. If I was still with my stbxH [soon to be ex-husband], I'd still be doing all the work, but not get the credit. Maybe that is petty, but I work hard raising my sons to be good people—good MEN—and I think it is important for the world to know that a single mom *can* raise good men. I make most all of the decisions to the well-being of my child, and I do not have to go through another person every time I want to do something.
- No confusion over discipline techniques.
- If I do not want my son to have something, so be it.
- I love that I get to be sandwiched between two little boys to sleep.
- Anytime the kids find an injured animal or bring home a stray, I can say "yes."
- I love that I can parent basically any way I want.
- I don't have to put up with some asshole telling me to "toughen up" my 6-week-old son by letting him cry.
- My 7-year-old doesn't get flack for sleeping in the family bed.
- My time at home is focused 100 percent on Alex. I don't have to worry about balancing a needy husband, and a needy toddler.
- 8YO son can dress however he wants, without being teased. Oh, I could go on and on. Oh, I love being single!!

- I love that I have no guilt about not spending "enough time" with him or "too much time" with the kids.
- When the Dumplings find a stray kitten, I can say "of course."
- "We" don't get in trouble for being loud and obnoxious!!!!
- Never having to justify why I am breastfeeding for as long as my little one needs/wants to to someone who feels he has the right to stop me.
- Alex has been running around lately with a pink feather boa around his neck . . . and there is no one here to make stupid comments or say he looks "gay" like I know my ex would have done. We are free to be ourselves 100 percent and that is priceless.
- No more being scrunched between a snoring husband and a wiggly baby.
- Dancing and singing around the house. I love that my sons now know that whatever they feel, wear, play with, or say is fine and no one in their home will judge them for it.
- I know that he will truly grow up to be who he wants to be (no one saying boys don't cry or boys don't do that)—those are some reasons I love being a single mom but there are so many more!!!!
- Co-sleeping with my babies can happen as long as it needs to.
- I don't have to watch him rush her to the ER for every freakin' sniffle.
- Co-sleeping with my daughter (who has always slept soundly all night as long as she can have a hand or foot touching me). Extended breastfeeding. No one to second-guess my decision to not vaccinate her (the result of reading many books and articles). Likewise my decisions about nutrition, i.e., no dairy or sugar, little meat (again, the result of a lot of thought and research, trying to think outside the box). No TV. No one to compromise her well-being physically or emotionally. We play together and work together around the house. We hike, we camp, we beachcomb, we read, we make art together, we have FUN. No one else to take up my attention and emotional energy—yet we have lots of close friends and family in our lives and in our home, so my daughter also knows how to be part of a larger group and is not growing up thinking the world is centered around her. I am mindful and grateful for every day we continue in good health and safety. All the work I have put into my own emotional healing and growth

is paying off a thousandfold in my conscious parenting. Hopefully, my daughter will step into the world from where I am now. She will have issues, but I pray they are different issues than what I grew up with. The no-dad thing will be one of them—but since I don't feel deprived by not having a partner, at least she won't pick up that vibe from me.

- We (myself and my ex) could never have been the parents we are today if we would have stayed together. For some reason we couldn't support each other . . . we got in each other's way. Now that we're apart our kids have a great mom and a great dad who can focus on them instead of their messed-up marriage.

ON MONEY

- No one running up my cell phone bill calling some other girl.
- No worries about getting to the grocery store only to find that the bank account was drained. I am responsible for all money and don't have to justify anything to anyone.
- No more hiding my bank ATM/debit card or changing the PIN weekly so cash can't be taken out.
- No complaints about how I spend money.
- All the bills get paid on time.
- His money problems will be just that HIS PROBLEMS, not ours.
- My kids and I actually dress way nicer now and eat better than I did when I was married, even though our income is miniscule (especially compared to what my ex made).
- I love the stability I now have knowing that I am in control of what money comes into this house, and how it is spent, knowing it isn't going to disappear or be spent on alcohol, big-screen TVs, or "unaccountable" purchases.
- I can buy/not buy anything I want . . . my money (what little I have ☺) is 100 percent my own now!
- I'm grateful not to be dragging a man through this recession. Worrying about his ego, building him up, dealing with his various small meannesses and rationalizing them as his worrying about us, fighting over how to handle a long dry spell for money. I'm relieved not to be playing the game where you carry the man but pretend he's your protector, and cling to him. In my house,

the recession is an opportunity to start showing dd [dear daughter] around the land of work, money, economics, home economy, tzedakah, personal responsibility, justice, and mercy. She's only five, but she understands that when people lose jobs, they can't buy stuff, and then what happens to the stores? And the people who work there? And so on. What about these people who lost their homes, whom should we help, and why? What about those who got themselves in trouble? What about their kids? Etc.

ON APPEARANCES

- When my ex left he took all the junk food with him and I lost and have kept off about 35 pounds.
- I can wear the most tacky pink fake satin robe and fuzzy slippers without anyone critiquing my fashion sense except my boys who think I look like a princess.
- Can I just say how great it is to be able to file dead skin off my feet whenever and wherever I want?
- One thing that really bothered me about cohabitation is how annoyed men are about being "subjected" to our beauty rituals . . . yet they want us to look/feel/smell good all the damn time.
- Eating pasta with anchovies and pickled garlic for dinner and not even brushing my teeth afterwards!
- I don't have to shave anything to feel pretty ☺.
- Not being cheated on or being dumped on for having post-baby body.
- I no longer feel the need to suck in my gut.
- I almost never feel fat, even though I am.
- I never have to suck in my stomach.
- If I do not feel like taking a shower, I never get teased.
- No one to tell me that I should have my breasts lifted after breast-feeding.
- I love the fact that no one borrows my razor ☺ . . . I love the fact that I don't feel any pressure to use that razor ☺.
- I can buy chocolate at will.
- I can get my hair cut as short as I like, or as "masculine"-looking as I want. Right now I'm sporting Joan Jett. And I LOVE it.

- No feeling guilty/unattractive/fat/whatever when we don't have sex.
- If I feel like spending all day Saturday in my pjs, I can without hearing "Are you going to get dressed SOMETIME today?!"
- I feel beautiful again for the first time since having my first child.
- And I feel healthier.

ON FAMILY AND FRIENDS

- I do not have to be nice to [mother-in-law] anymore!! I don't have to put up with her crap and can tell her to shove it if I want to! I don't have to go there ever again.
- No husband = no in-laws . . .
- I love that I can pick my friends freely without worrying about my partner's judgments.
- I love having friends and not worrying that someone is jealous about it.
- I get to go out with my friends.
- I get to HAVE friends!
- I can have friends spend the night, weekend, month.
- I can be close to my family again; they hated him.
- I can go spend 3 weeks w/ my family!
- Because we are now free to develop relationships and networks of healthy, whole, loving people to support and care for us and have fun with us.
- My kids will finally get to meet my family members they've never even met.
- I get to hang w/ my family more often (and don't have endure endless calls from stbx asking when I'll be home). No one here turns up their noses at healthy organic foods.
- I have been able to have my 85-year-old mom come live with me.

ON ROMANCE AND DATING

- Being a single mom has allowed me to be in a wonderful, healthy, loving relationship with a great man. Creating the kind of relationship I deserve and could never have had with my ex.

- I'm a single mom who now has a partner who's loving and supportive and helpful and supports who I am and how I raise my kid.
- I am so in love, so happy now. A year ago I would have told you no way, I am done with men. And here I am 9 months into an incredibly happy relationship. . . . By getting rid of the old I was able to move on to the new. I wasn't expecting to find it. But I did. And girlfriends, believe me when I tell you: the new is very, very good indeed.
- I can have sex with other men, whenever I want, for however long I feel like without my genitals being owned by anyone. I am not tied down or locked into place until I die.
- You can drool over all the hot guys you want to.

ON DISCOVERING THE TIGER

- I have so much pride that I support them by myself. Everyone talks about how hard single parenting is. Are you kidding me? It's so much easier!
- The satisfaction of knowing that I can and am doing this all alone, that I am strong enough to do so; like most female mammals this planet has ever known, I raise the young on my own without male help.
- I loved finding out how truly strong I was inside, and learning that I am lovable, I am worthy of being loved, and learning to love me all over again.
- I loved being dependent on ME and only me for everything.
- Knowing that when the pipes burst in the bathroom *I can fix it*!
- I love looking forward to the future and knowing the really hard times (dealing with abuse, court battles, ugly dramas, and empty fridge days) are in the past. I love imagining how I can further transform our lives for the better!
- I feel so empowered knowing that "I" replaced the broken phone jack, lit the pilot light on the water heater, hung the shelves, got the kitchen window to close, etc., etc., etc. Installing a light fixture is next on my list.
- I loved succeeding when my ex was sure I would fall flat on my ass.
- It's harder, but being a single mother has changed me for the better. I am so much stronger now.

- *I* fixed the furnace! *I* managed to keep us $afloat$! *I* gave her that confidence and security! *I* know exactly what cool activity she'd love this weekend, and get us in free! *I* found and nurtured her musical talent!

- My daughter needed a dresser, we bought one at Ikea and did a perfect job of putting it together. WOO HOO. I also had Internet hooked up and set up a wireless network all by myself. I thought I needed a guy for those sorts of things but I can do it myself!! And have a great time doing it!

- Just back from a fantastic 3-day camping trip with just me and the kids. Swimming, hiking, pony rides, fun . . . No negotiations, no bickering, simplicity and peace. We all had a fantastic time, met tons of people that we wouldn't have if ex was there (not the most social guy), I remembered again I'm capable of so much more than it seemed when we were together, the kids were easy easy to deal with the whole time, I was so relaxed, and I got my own campfire going!

- I don't have to waste any of my precious time on this earth complaining about some man and what he has or hasn't done.

- I love that I am finally growing a backbone.

- I love how powerful and competent I feel, knowing I'm doing a very tough job all by myself, completely solo, and that we're THRIVING.

- All of the most excellent women I know are single moms!

ON HAPPINESS

- I love that [my kids] don't feel like they need to help Mommy because she's sad.

- My kids have a happy mom.

- I am less lonely than I was during my marriage.

- I know that my son will always be in a happy, loving home.

- I love that I am so connected to my dd [dear daughter]. It's something that people notice about us all the time. The only way I could ever have had this bond was because I was single and never had to worry about anyone else except my dd [dear daughter].

- Sometimes SINGLE isn't so much the goal as "not with someone horrible." Single is WAY better than a bad marriage.

- My son and I are both so much healthier than we were with his father.
- I love being a single mother because my children see my light-filled striving (even when I feel like I'm failing) and they appreciate me for my love, my time, and my heartful efforts to make our lives beautiful. They know I do double and then some. I love the common understanding we three hold that I am capable, strong, and guiding our ship onwards and upwards.
- I'm not short tempered with DD [dear daughter].
- My children's dad is now my friend instead of my foe.
- My kids are growing up in a happy home.
- My son would never get the sort of attention I can give him now. The joy and confidence my son has are so precious and it gives *me* joy knowing I did the right thing for him (and me). (And yes, the financial stuff can be overwhelming, but if you have enough to get by, that's all you need. A child's health and well-being can't be given a price.)
- I belong to other parenting forums and some of them sort of "look down" (to a degree) on single mothers, or I see many references of, "thank goodness I have my DH [dear husband] because I could NEVER be a single mom! I don't know how they do it!" Now I realize it's their opinion, but I can't help but feel a little upset when people say things like this. For me, it was the best thing that has ever happened to me and I am PROUD to be a single mom.
- Everyone in my home is cherished and respected.
- I am overflowing with self-respect, self-worth, independence, happiness, and love.
- I can take all the credit when someone says "ohhh, what a happy baby he is!"
- My brain doesn't feel foggy all time. My memory is better. I have energy. I'm HAPPY!

ON OUR POWER TO CHANGE THE WORLD

- One thing I love about being a single mama is that my boys are growing up and they're turning out to be such wonderful people. I know that I alone have done 99 percent of the work involved.

I can look at them every day and be proud that they are who they are because of me.

- I love that my kids no longer see Teenage Mutant Ninja turtles or The Simpsons on a daily basis and I don't have to constantly argue why that is not good for them.
- I love the fact the kids will KNOW I did this on my own. I hope it makes them stronger people because of it.
- I get to show my boys that girls can fix things with screwdrivers.
- There will never be a hunting rifle or gun of any nature in my house.
- My kids aren't seeing a poor example of what a marriage (theoretically) can be.
- My son will be raised with my values, not my in-laws'.
- You know your child won't be exposed to endless hours of annoying video games.
- My kids know that girls can use tools and fix things, too.
- Every chore in the house can become gender neutral.
- My kid can be a tree hugger, just like his mama.
- No sports on TV, no shoot-'em-up explosion death and mayhem TV shows or video games in my home. No football or war movies or stereotypical male entertainment in my household.
- I've raised my son in a family where honesty, respect, and caring are the central tenets of his home—so what if it was a family of two? I'm seeing the results in a wonderful, open, funny, sweet 16-year-old boy.
- I am **single**, **happy**, and **proud** of it because overall I know that if I am a good influence on [her] she has a damn good chance of becoming a great person that feels great about who she is and the life she lives.
- Raising my son with good values and positive male role models (my dad and other men in our family).
- I love being able to express my thoughts and feelings about stuff with my kids and having them able to do likewise.
- I love that I will give him a great woman model to look to . . . I love this. Not a suffered woman, not one who is fighting and grumpy all day. A soul-free woman.
- I know that he will grow up to respect women.

- My son will know how women are SUPPOSED to be treated!
- I love that I can teach my son to be respectful of all living creatures, regardless of gender, race, species, color, etc.

ON SELF-ESTEEM

- Nobody thinks my beliefs are silly or stupid.
- No one is calling me an idiot.
- No one to put me down!!!
- I love that I can let my light shine without stifling it to not make my partner feel insecure.
- I like that there's no one around to make me feel insufficient.
- I loved regaining my self-esteem and finding out who I am after being mistreated for so long.
- I have become very resourceful.
- No one to bash me as a STAM [stay-at-home mom] ('cause you know we all just sit around all day, watch TV, and eat bonbons ☺).
- I love that I don't have to endure put-downs in front of my son.
- P.S. I've been on my own for 11 years now but this is the first time that I am the only adult of the household. This is my home, just mine. I'm really proud that I have my own home & share it with 3 of the greatest little people on the planet.
- Looking back I am proud of my accomplishments as a mother and a woman. We are not a statistic (single mother on welfare, delinquent kid). D's a good student and an amazing kid. I still get a hug and kiss before he takes the bus to school.
- I also love that I don't have to feel like a failure because he is.
- It is amazing, isn't it? I feel better now, almost exactly 1 year later, than I did during what was supposed to be the "happiest time of my life—just had a baby and planning a wedding).
- Knowing that despite the system's often disparaging and punitive attitude towards some moms that I have done this incredible feat ON MY OWN [and] therefore I've accomplished something great when I was told I would amount to nothing at all.

ON MUSIC

- I get to choose the music.
- I can sing the most irritating falsetto opera in the house, without any inhibitions.
- We sing all the time with nobody getting annoyed.
- Listening to radio Disney in the car and not being embarrassed that I know the words to most of the songs.
- I can play whatever music I want as loud as I want. Even the "weird" stuff.

ON GRATITUDE

- What a blessing to have had no choice but to find the strength/patience/humility/resilience/energy/resourcefulness/courage necessary to do it alone within myself. That's why I love being a single mother.
- I LOVE this thread! I re-read it every now and then, and even if I don't chime in, y'all remind me to appreciate the wonderful life my Dumplings and I have. Today my 8YO Dumpling wrote a poem their dad would never have appreciated:

    There are icicles on the bicycles, and frost is on the grass.
    If I went for a walk on the ice, I'd slip and fall on my . . . . . .
                        hands and knees.

ON SIMPLICITY

- The wonderful adventures that are so easy for twosomes (of whatever age, including two adults) and so hard for more-than-two (with everyone's disparate schedules & moods). Last night we went to a local beach for a bonfire and caroling by the docking "Christmas ships"; so cool! Can't imagine my stuffy ex going for something that pedestrian! And this weekend we might drive into the mountains just to see snow, because why not? Wa-hoo!
- I love that we no longer have to give in to materialism, and that my children will grow up understanding the principle of voluntary simplicity.

ON FREEDOM

- I love that we can eat, sleep, & do whatever we want basically anytime we want.
- I can stop feeling like I need to wait for his permission, or blessing, to live my life. I can give **myself** permission to live.
- I get to pick the meals all the time.
- I love that I can study, read, or watch anything on TV at night.
- I can paint my bedroom walls burgundy.
- I make all my own decisions. My life is my own.
- We can cultivate our own traditions without anyone mocking them.
- I never have to watch another violent movie.
- I can paint the kitchen walls salmon. I mean bright. Really bright.
- I can shop when I want and get what I want without having anyone give me the silent third degree.
- I get to say who's in my house.
- The spiders I find occasionally in the house don't get squished, they get put out the window.
- I get to do what I want, when I want.
- I can decorate the apartment as I see fit for the holidays.
- No football ever!!! No ESPN!!! No wrestling, no stupid movies filled with fighting and cursing.
- I can spend 5+ hours on the computer, reading a magazine, or on the phone at night without being given a hard time (when I know if I was on the couch, I'd be ignored anyway).
- The big big big big thing for me—and, I see, for many of you—is making the decisions. Whether it's having the power to color-coordinate the kitchen, or to decide [other aspects of life] it's a wonderful luxury.
- I'm freeeeeeeeeee!

ON BEING MYSELF

- I can change and grow as much as I want.
- I'm learning a lot about myself that I probably wouldn't have otherwise.

- I have time and energy and motivation to figure out my life without being distracted or having someone else's opinion affecting my decisions.
- I am more politically aware without having to debate all my thoughts.
- Being able to change my whole life and worldview as I read and explore more and encounter such wisdom and depth in areas I'd never even considered before. (My ex hated how changeable I can be—seeing it as inconsistent rather than fluid.)
- I never have to say, "I wish I could ____, but my husband won't let me/doesn't like it."
- I don't need permission to do ANYTHING. I live on my own terms.
- I am in control of my own destiny. I can change my course as I choose without being accused of being indecisive.
- I love being able to have my own traditions.
- I am more compassionate for my fellow human beings.
- I can really appreciate an hour alone in a cafe.
- I love being able to change.
- Best of all, you have self-respect!
- I can have as many cats as I want.
- When someone says to me "ohhh, I wish I could do that, but my husband won't let me." It always makes me smile and chuckle a little because I know I can do whatever I want and no one can say I can't.

AND FINALLY, AN INVOCATION

"Blessings to all the single mothers. May we all have the strength to love and live to the fullest each day and all the patience to succeed at one of the most demanding jobs, which never ends and no one ever takes over for second shift."

Series Afterword by Michele A. Paludi

It's not only children who grow. Parents do too. As much as we watch to see what our children do with their lives, they are watching us to see what we do with ours. I can't tell my children to reach for the sun. All I can do is reach for it, myself.

—Joyce Maynard

Maynard's sentiment is captured in Sandy Chalkoun's book, *Single Mother in Charge: How to Successfully Pursue Happiness.* Chalkoun dispels myths of single parenting for women in a developmental fashion: from the time a woman finds herself a single mother to finding herself again as an individual. She traces steps women must take to *value and love ourselves* for who we are—not only in terms of our relationships with friends, romantic partners, children, employers, co-workers, and parents—but ourselves, single or married, separated or divorced, able bodied or disabled, parent or no parent, overweight or underweight, and working inside or outside the home. Chalkoun offers recommendations for empowering single mothers, not reinforcing stereotypes that blame women for the end of their marriages or for raising children alone without a father. She highlights research results that indicate that what is most important for children is not that they are raised in any specific family structure, but rather how effective the relationship is with the single parent, the support they are getting from this parent, and whether their home environment is encouraging and valuing.

Chalkoun captures the essence of Praeger's Women's Psychology series: facilitating connections between readers' experiences, psychological theories, empirical research, and in this case positive psychology. She provides readers with opportunities to challenge their views about women, men, marriage, parenting, and self-concept. Readers of this book will derive strength from Chalkoun's efforts and the efforts of others she cites who have worked for social change on the interpersonal level.

Notes

SECTION 1

1. S. Wolf, "Effects of Suggestion and Conditioning on the Action of Chemical Agents in Human Subjects: The Pharmacology of Placebos," *Journal of Clinical Investigation* 29 (1950): 100–9, http://www.jci.org/articles/view/102225. Last accessed March 7, 2010.

2. Ibid.

3. Herbert Benson and Richard Friedman, "Harnessing the Power of the Placebo Effect and Renaming It Remembered Wellness," *Annual Review of Medicine* 47 (1996): 193–99, http://arjournals.annualreviews.org/doi/abs/10.1146/annurev.med.47.1.193?. Last accessed on March 5, 2010.

4. Irving Hirsch, "Antidepressants: The Emperor's New Drugs?" *The Huffington Post*, January 29, 2010. http://www.huffingtonpost.com/irving-kirsch-phd/antidepressants-the-emper_b_442205.html. Last accessed March 8, 2010.

5. "National Patterns in Antidepressant Medication Treatment," *Archives of General Psychiatry* Vol. 66, http://archpsyc.ama-assn.org/cgi/content/abstract/66/8/848. Last accessed March 8, 2010.

6. Rebecca L. Waver, Baba Shiv, Ziv Carmon, and Dan Ariely, "Commercial Features of Placebo and Therapeutic Efficacy," *Journal of the American Medical Association* 299, no. 9 (2008), http://jama.ama-assn.org/cgi/content/full/299/9/1016. Last accessed March 8, 2010.

7. Mark Pratt, "Ig Nobel Winners Honoured," *The Globe and Mail*, October 3, 2008, http://www.theglobeandmail.com/news/technology/article713578.ece. Last accessed March 8, 2010.

8. Brian Reid, "The Nocebo Effect: Placebo's Evil Twin," *The Washington Post*, April 30, 2002, http://www.washingtonpost.com/ac2/wp-dyn/A2709-2002Apr29. Last accessed March 10, 2010.

9. Wikipedia, "Nocebo," http://en.wikipedia.org/wiki/Nocebo. Last accessed March 10, 2010.

10. Reid, "The Nocebo Effect."

11. Ibid.

12. Wikipedia, "Albert Einstein," http://simple.wikipedia.org/wiki/Albert_Einstein. Last accessed March 10, 2010.

13. Mark Easton, "The Health Benefits of Happiness," BBC News, May 23, 2006, http://news.bbc.co.uk/2/hi/programmes/happiness_formula/4924180.stm. Last accessed March 10, 2010; Deborah D. Danner, David A. Snowdon, and Wallace V. Friesen, "Positive emotions in early life and longevity: Findings from the nun study," *Journal of Personality and Social Psychology*. Vol 80(5), May 2001, 804–13. http://www.students.sbc.edu/leasetrevathan06/Danner%20Reading.pdf. Last accessed March 12, 2010.

14. "Smoker's Life Span," Web MD, http://www.webmd.com/hw-popup/smokings-impact-on-life-span. Last accessed March 10, 2010.

15. David G. Myers, *Psychology*, 9th ed. (New York: Worth, 2010), 520, http://www.davidmyers.org/davidmyers/assets/9e-Happiness.pdf. Last accessed March 10, 2010.

16. Christopher Petersen, *A Primer in Positive Psychology* (New York: Oxford University Press, 2006), 114.

17. Easton, "The Health Benefits of Happiness."

18. Karen Weekes, *"Women Know Everything!": 3,241 Quips, Quotes, and Brilliant Remarks* (Philadelphia: Quirk Books, 2007), 10.

SECTION 2

1. Jiddu Krishnamurti, *The Collected Works of J. Krishnamurti: A Psychological Revolution*, vol. 13 (Dubuque, IA: Kendall/Hunt, 1962–1963), 240.

2. Bstan-dzin-rgya-mtsho (Dalai Lama XIV) and Howard C. Cutler, *The Art of Happiness: A Handbook for Living* (New York: Riverhead Books, 1998), 38.

3. "Mark Twain Quotes," *Brainy Quote*, http://www.brainyquote.com/quotes/quotes/m/marktwain141714.html. Last accessed March 10, 2010.

4. Gavin de Becker, *The Gift of Fear* (Canada: Little, Brown, 1997), 2.

5. Ibid., 28.

6. A View on Buddhism, "Quotations on: Fear, Anxiety," http://www.viewonbuddhism.org/dharma-quotes-quotations-buddhist/fear-anxiety.htm. Last accessed March 10, 2010.

7. Wikiquote, "E. E. Cummings," http://en.wikiquote.org/wiki/E._E._Cummings. Last accessed March 10, 2010.

8. J. Gouin, J. Kiecolt-Glaser, W. Malarkey, and R. Glaser, "The Influence of Anger Expression on Wound Healing," *Brain, Behavior, and*

Immunity 22, no. 5 (2008): 699–708, http://www.ncbi.nlm.nih.gov/pmc/articles/PMC2502071/. Last accessed March 10, 2010.

9. Lindsay Lyon, "Want to Be Happier? Here's How," *U.S. News and World Report*, January 18, 2008, Health Section. http://health.usnews.com/articles/health/2008/01/18/want-to-be-happier-heres-how.html. Last accessed March 10, 2010.

10. A View on Buddhism, "Anger and Aversion," http://viewonbuddhism.org/anger.html

11. Quote Garden, "Quotations about Anger," http://www.quotegarden.com/anger.html. Last accessed March 10, 2010.

12. "Major JRF Study Reviews Experiences of Children Whose Parents Divorce," Joseph Rowntree Foundation online database, June 1, 1998, http://www.jrf.org.uk/media-centre/major-jrf-study-reviews-experiences-children-whose-parents-divorce. Last accessed March 10, 2010.

13. Nancy E. Dowd, *In Defense of Single-Parent Families* (New York: New York University Press, 1997), xix.

14. "Add Health," Carolina Population Center online database, http://www.cpc.unc.edu/projects/addhealth. Last accessed March 10, 2010.

15. R. W. Blum, T. Beuhring, M. L. Shew, L. H. Bearinger, R. E. Sieving, and M. D. Resnick, "The Effects of Race/Ethnicity, Income, and Family Structure on Adolescent Risk Behaviors," *American Journal of Public Health* 90, no. 12 (2000): 1879–84, http://www.ncbi.nlm.nih.gov/pmc/articles/PMC1446419/pdf/11111260.pdf. Last accessed March 10, 2010.

16. Dennis Saleebey, *Strengths Perspective in Social Work Practice* (Boston: Allyn & Bacon, 2006), 204, https://www.wested.org/chks/pdf/strengths_perspective.pdf. Last accessed March 12, 2010.

17. "Adolescent Health," Australian Broadcasting Corporation, program transcript, September 22, 1997, http://www.abc.net.au/rn/talks/8.30/helthrpt/stories/s267.htm. Last accessed March 10, 2010.

18. "On Mother's Day, a Hopeful Finding for Single Mothers and Their Children from a Cornell Researcher," *Cornell News*, May 6, 2004, http://www.news.cornell.edu/releases/May04/single.parents.ssl.html. Last accessed March 10, 2010.

19. Ibid.

20. Ibid.

21. Ibid.

22. Saleebey, *Strengths Perspective*.

23. "Time Single Working Moms Spend with Kids Surprises Researchers," University of Maryland Newsdesk, November 25, 2008, http://www.newsdesk.umd.edu/mail/send.cfm?articleID=1795. Last accessed March 10, 2010.

24. B. R. Levy, M. D. Slade, S. R. Kunkel, and S. V. Kasl, "Longevity increased by positive self-perceptions of aging," *Journal of Personality and*

Social Psychology Vol 83(2), August 2002, 261–70, http://psycnet.apa.org/index.cfm?fa=buy.optionToBuy&id=2002-17391-001&CFID=6796644&CFTOKEN=95555012. Last accessed March 12, 2010.

25. Maia Szalavitz, "Today Show Revises the Number of Missing Kids Downward," STATS, March 9, 2006, http://www.stats.org/stories/2006/Today_missing_kids_mar09_06.htm. Last accessed March 10, 2010; "Statistics," National Center for Missing and Exploited Children online database, http://www.missingkids.com/missingkids/servlet/PageServlet?LanguageCountry=en_US&PageId=2810. Last accessed March 10, 2010.

26. Gerd Gigerenzer, Wolfgang Gaissmaier, Elke Kurz-Milcke, Lisa M. Schwartz, and Steven Woloshin, "Knowing Your Chances: What Health Stats Really Mean," *Scientific American Mind*, April 2009.

27. Saleebey, *Strengths Perspective*.

28. "Michel de Montaigne," Wikiquote, http://en.wikiquote.org/wiki/Michel_de_Montaigne.

29. "Shantideva," Wikiquote, http://en.wikiquote.org/wiki/Shantideva.

30. David G. Myers, "The Secrets of Happiness," *Psychology Today*, July 1, 1992, http://www.psychologytoday.com/articles/199207/the-secrets-happiness. Last accessed March 10, 2010.

31. "The Problem with Self-Help Books: Study Shows the Negative Side to Positive Self-Statements," news release, Association for Psychological Science, July 2, 2009, http://www.psychologicalscience.org/media/releases/2009/wood.cfm. Last accessed March 10, 2010; Joanne V. Wood, W.Q. Elaine Perunovic, and John W. Lee, "Positive Self-Statements: Power for Some, Peril for Others," *Psychological Science*, Vol. 20, No. 7, pp. 860–66. http://www3.interscience.wiley.com/journal/122399441/abstract?CRETRY=1&SRETRY=0. Last accessed March 10, 2010.

32. Ibid.

33. BrainyQuote, "Anita Roddick Quotes," http://www.brainyquote.com/quotes/authors/a/anita_roddick.html. Last accessed March 10, 2010.

34. BrainyQuote, "Vincent van Gogh Quotes," http://www.brainyquote.com/quotes/quotes/v/vincentvan104644.html. Last accessed March 10, 2010

35. John L. Gittleman, "Female Brain Size and Parental Care in Carnivores," *Proceedings of the National Academy of Science USA* 91 (1994): 5495–97, http://www.pnas.org/content/91/12/5495.full.pdf. Last accessed March 10, 2010.

36. Wisdom Quotes, http://www.wisdomquotes.com/001835.html. Last accessed March 10, 2010.

37. Martin E. P. Seligman, "Learned Helplessness," *Annual Review of Medicine* 23 (1972): 407–12, http://arjournals.annualreviews.org/doi/abs/10.1146/annurev.me.23.020172.002203?cookieSet=1&journalCode=med. Last accessed March 10, 2010; Seligman, *Learned Optimism: How to Change Your Mind and Your Life* (New York: Vintage Books, 2006), 19.

SECTION 3

1. Myers, *Psychology*, 522.

2. Wikipedia, "Psychology of Happiness," http://www.scholarpedia.org/article/Psychology_of_happiness. Last accessed March 10, 2010; Myers, "Pursuing Happiness," *Psychology Today*, July 1, 1993, http://www.psychologytoday.com/articles/199307/pursuing-happiness. Last accessed March 10, 2010.

3. National Institute of Mental Health, "Statistics." http://www.nimh.nih.gov/health/topics/statistics/index.shtml. Last accessed March 10, 2010.

4. Myers, *Psychology*.

5. "Remarks of Senator Barack Obama," Campus Progress Annual Conference, Washington, DC, July 12, 2006, http://www.barackobama.com/2006/07/12/campus_progress_annual_conference.php. Last accessed March 10, 2010.

6. Tim Kasser, "Materialism and Its Alternatives," in *A Life Worth Living: Contributions to Positive Psychology*, ed. Mihaly Csikszentmihalyi and Isabella Selega Csikszentmihalyi (New York: Oxford University Press, 2006), 202.

7. David Myers, "The Secret to Happiness," *Yes!* June 18, 2004, http://www.yesmagazine.org/issues/what-is-the-good-life/866; Myers, *Psychology*, 523.

8. Myers, "Pursuing Happiness."

9. Ibid.

10. J. K. Boehm and S. Lyubomirsky, "The Promise of Sustainable Happiness," in *Handbook of Positive Psychology*, C. R. Snyder and Shane J. Lopez, 9 (Oxford: Oxford University Press, 2009), http://www.faculty.ucr.edu/~sonja/papers/BLinpressa.pdf. Last accessed March 10, 2010; P. Brickman, D. Coates, and R. Janoff-Bulman, "Lottery Winners and Accident Victims: Is Happiness Relative?" *Journal of Personality and Social Psychology* 36 (1978): 917–27, http://www.ncbi.nlm.nih.gov/pubmed/690806.

11. "Are Married People Happier Than Unmarried People?" APA Online, March 16, 2003, http://www.apa.org/releases/married_happy.html. Last accessed March 10, 2010.

12. Ibid.

13. Myers, "Pursuing Happiness."

14. NielsenWire, "Women's Happiness More Recession Proof than Men's," November 26, 2008, http://blog.nielsen.com/nielsenwire/global/womens-happiness-more-recession-proof-than-mens/. Last accessed March 10, 2010.

15. Sonja Lyubomirsky, *The How of Happiness* (New York: Penguin Press, 2007), 47.

16. "Achieving Fame, Wealth, and Beauty are Psychological Dead Ends, Study Says," University of Rochester, May 19, 2009, http://www.rochester.edu/news/show.php?id=3377. Last accessed April 28, 2010.

17. "Authentic Happiness: Using Our Strengths to Cultivate Happiness," ABCNews.com, 2002, http://abcnews.go.com/GMA/story?id=125797&page=2. Last accessed March 11, 2010.

18. Boehm and Lyubomirsky, "The Promise of Sustainable Happiness."

SECTION 4

1. Seligman, *Learned Optimism*.

2. Ibid., 16.

3. Ibid., 8.

4. Ibid., 30.

5. Ibid., 15.

6. Seligman, *Learned Optimism*, 44ff; Wikipedia, "Explanatory Style," http://en.wikipedia.org/wiki/Explanatory_style. Last accessed March 11, 2010.

7. Seligman, *Learned Optimism*.

8. "Depression Linked to Bone-Thinning in Premenopausal Women," National Institute of Mental Health, press release, November 26, 2007, http://www.nimh.nih.gov/science-news/2007/depression-linked-to-bone-thinning-in-premenopausal-women.shtml. Last accessed March 11, 2010.

9. Martin E. P. Seligman, *The Optimistic Child* (New York: Houghton Mifflin, 2007), 293.

10. "Cancer Climber Association," www.CancerClimber.com. Last accessed March 11, 2010.

11. "Helen Keller," Wikiquote, http://en.wikiquote.org/wiki/Helen_Keller. Last accessed March 11, 2010.

12. Maryann Bird, "Nothing Like A Dame," *Time*, October 2, 2004, http://www.time.com/time/europe/hero2004/roddick.html. Last accessed March 11, 2010.

13. "Money Buys Happiness When You Spend on Others: UBC and Harvard Research," University of British Columbia, media release, March 20, 2008, http://www.publicaffairs.ubc.ca/media/releases/2008/mr-08-032.html. Last accessed March 11, 2010.

14. "Mihaly Csikszentmihalyi on Flow," TED: Ideas Worth Spreading, http://www.ted.com/talks/mihaly_csikszentmihalyi_on_flow.html. Last accessed March 11, 2010.

15. Wikipedia, "Bhutan," http://en.wikipedia.org/wiki/Bhutan. Last accessed March 11, 2010.

16. Jeff Greenwald, "Happy Land," *Yoga Journal*, November 2003, http://www.yogajournal.com/lifestyle/1332. Last accessed March 11, 2010.

17. "Bhutan's Happiness Formula," BBC News, April 27, 2006, http://news.bbc.co.uk/1/hi/in_pictures/4782636.stm. Last accessed March 11, 2010.

18. Andrew C. Revkin, "A New Measure of Well-Being from a Happy Little Kingdom," *The New York Times*, October 4, 2005, http://www.nytimes.com/2005/10/04/science/04happ.html?pagewanted=all. Last accessed March 11, 2010.

19. Kahlil Gibran, *The Prophet* (Middlesex: The Ecco Library, 2006), 8.

20. "Johann Wolfgang von Goethe Quotes," BrainyQuote, http://www.brainyquote.com/quotes/quotes/j/johannwolf169653.html.

21. Lyubomirsky, *The How of Happiness*, 90.

22. Robert Emmons, *Thanks!: How the New Science of Gratitude Can Make You Happier* (New York: Houghton Mifflin Company, 2007).

23. Claudia Wallis, "The New Science of Happiness," *Time*, January 17, 2005, http://www.authentichappiness.sas.upenn.edu/images/TimeMagazine/Time-Happiness.pdf. Last accessed March 11, 2010.

24. Emmons, *Thanks!: How the New Science of Gratitude Can Make You Happier*, 12.

25. "Benjamin Franklin," Wikiquote http://en.wikiquote.org/wiki/Benjamin_Franklin. Last accessed March 11, 2010.

26. "For The Average British Woman, Life In A Couple Means More Housework And Less Wellbeing" *The Economic Journal*, 2007, http://www.Res.Org.Uk/Society/Mediabriefings/Pdfs/2007/0701/Couprie.Asp. Last accessed March 11, 2010.

27. Barry Schwartz, *The Paradox of Choice: Why More Is Less* (New York: HarperCollins, 2004).

28. Schwartz, "Swarthmore Last Collection," *Authentic Happiness*, May 29, 2004, http://www.authentichappiness.sas.upenn.edu/newsletter.aspx?id=46. Last accessed March 11, 2010.

29. Schwartz, "Can There Ever Be Too Many Flowers Blooming?" in *Engaging Art: The Next Great Transformation of America's Cultural Life*, ed. W. Ivey and S. J. Tepper (New York: Routledge, 2007), http://www.swarthmore.edu/SocSci/bschwar1/SchwartzCulture.pdf. Last accessed March 10, 2010.

30. Boehm and Lyubomirsky, "The Promise of Sustainable Happiness," 6; B. Schwartz, A. Ward, J. Monterosso, S. Lyubomirsky, K. White, and D. R. Lehman, "Maximizing Versus Satisficing: Happiness Is a Matter of Choice," *Journal of Personality and Social Psychology* 83, no. 5 (2002): 117897, http://www.swarthmore.edu/SocSci/bschwar1/maximizing.pdf. Last accessed March 11, 2010.

31. Schwartz, "Swarthmore Last Collection."

32. Boehm and Lyubomirsky, "The Promise of Sustainable Happiness," 6; Schwartz, Ward, Monterosso, Lyubomirsky, White, and Lehman, "Maximizing Versus Satisficing."

33. Schwartz, "Swarthmore Last Collection."

34. David Niven, *The 100 Simple Secrets of Happy People* (New York: HarperCollins, 2003), 104.

35. Catherine Guthrie, "Solve Problems in Your Sleep," *Prevention*, May 2006, 191, http://books.google.ca/books?id=TscDAAAAMBAJ&lpg =PA184&ots=WTcPUng5o3&dq=Robert%20Stickgold%20sleep%20is %20the%20glue%20that%20binds%20new%20information%20into%20the %20brain.&pg=PA191#v=onepage&q=Robert%20Stickgold%20sleep %20is%20the%20glue%20that%20binds%20new%20information%20into %20the%20brain.&f=false. Last accessed March 11, 2010.

36. "Stanford Study Links Obesity to Hormonal Changes from Lack of Sleep," Stanford University School of Medicine, news release, December 6, 2004, http://med.stanford.edu/news_releases/2004/December/mignot.htm. Last accessed March 10, 2010.

37. Julie Beun-Chown, "Dozing to Diet: Sleep as a Diet Aid Works, Research Shows," *Ottawa Citizen*, http://news.globaltv.com/health/Dozing +diet+Sleep+diet+works+research+shows/2009345/story.html. Last accessed March 11, 2010.

38. "So What Do You Have to Do to Find Happiness?" *Times Online*, October 2, 2005, http://www.employeeexcellence.com/LT.html. Last accessed March 11, 2010.

39. T. Särkämö, M. Tervaniemi, S. Laitinen, A. Forsblom, S. Soinila, M. Mikkonen, T. Autti, H. M. Silvennoinen, J. Erkkilä, M. Laine, I. Peretz, M. Hietanen. "Music listening enhances cognitive recovery and mood after middle cerebral artery stroke." *Brain*, March 2008; 131(Pt 3):866-76, http:// brain.oxfordjournals.org/cgi/content/abstract/131/3/866. Last accessed March 11, 2010; Michael Kahn, "Music Hits Right Notes for Stroke Patients," *Reuters*, February 19, 2008, http://www.reuters.com/article/healthNews/ idUSL1911114120080220. Last accessed March 15, 2010.

40. Tim Kasser, *The High Price of Materialism* (Achorn Graphic Services Inc., 2003), 103.

41. Wikipedia, "Norman Cousins," http://en.wikipedia.org/wiki/ Norman_Cousins. Last accessed March 11, 2010.

42. Bob Rosenbaum, "Norman Cousins Talks on Positive Emotions and Health," KCRW-FM, August 1983, transcription from the original radio broadcast, http://www.bobrosenbaum.com/transcripts/nctalks.pdf. Last accessed March 11, 2010.

43. Albert Nerenberg, "Laugh 'Til It Stops Hurting," *Montreal Gazette*, December 2, 2008, http://www2.canada.com/montrealgazette/features/ positivity/story.html?id=3860b4ee-58e5-4950-9c94-a2ffd1ce6754. Last accessed March 11, 2010.

44. Steve Ayan, "Laughing Matters," *Scientific American Mind*, April– June 2000, 26, http://tzenovs.com/SciAm/Mind/SAMind_200904.pdf. Last accessed March 11, 2010.

45. Ibid; Hajime Kimata, "Laughter elevates the levels of breast-milk melatonin," *Journal of Psychosomatic Research*—June 2007 (Vol. 62, No. 6, pp. 699–702, DOI: 10.1016/j.jpsychores.2006.12.007), http://

www.jpsychores.com/article/S0022-3999%2806%2900532-0/abstract. Last accessed March 15, 2010.

46. Hara Estroff Marano, "Move to Boost Mood," *Psychology Today*, November 1, 2001, http://www.psychologytoday.com/articles/pto-2914 .html. Last accessed March 11, 2010; "Exercise may be Just as Effective as Medication for Treating Major Depression" *Duke Medicine News and Communications*, October 24, 1999. http://www.dukehealth.org/health _library/news/300. Last accessed March 15, 2010.

47. Hara Estroff Marano, "Move to Boost Mood."

48. "New treatment hope for people with recurring depression" University of Exeter, http://www.exeter.ac.uk/news/research/title,1908,en.php. Last accessed March 11, 2010; Danny Penman, "Try Buddhism on Prescription to Tame Depression," *The Daily Telegraph*, December 5, 2008, http:// www.telegraph.co.uk/health/alternativemedicine/3568885/Try-Buddhism-on-prescription-to-tame-depression.html. Last accessed March 11, 2010.

49. Jon Kabat-Zinn, "Mindfulness Based Interventions in Context: Past, Present, and Future," *Clinical Psychology: Science and Practice* 10 (2003), http:// www.courses.fas.harvard.edu/~psy1504/AssignedReadings/Meditation -Review2.htm. Last accessed March 11, 2010.

50. Kathleen McGowan, "Loving the Lotus," *Psychology Today*, September 1, 2005, http://www.psychologytoday.com/articles/200508/loving-the-lotus. Last accessed March 11, 2010.

51. His Holiness the Dalai Lama, "The Monk in the Lab," *The New York Times*, April 26, 2003, http://www.lamayeshe.com/otherteachers/hhdl/ nyt_op_ed.shtml. Last accessed March 11, 2010. http://www.nytimes.com/ 2003/04/26/opinion/26LAMA.html?pagewanted=all. Last accessed March 10, 2010.

52. Ibid.

53. "Quotations about Silence," QuoteGarden, http://www.quote garden.com/silence.html. Last accessed March 11, 2010.

54. R. S. Ulrich, "View Through a Window May Influence Recovery from Surgery," *Science* 224, no. 4647 (1984), http://www.ncbi.nlm.nih.gov/ pubmed/6143402. Last accessed March 11, 2010.

55. "Executive Summary—Ecotherapy: The Green Agenda for Mental Health," *Mind Week Report*, May 2007, http://www.mind.org.uk/assets/ 0000/2139/ecotherapy_executivesummary.pdf. Last accessed March 15, 2010.

56. "Anne Frank," *Wikiquote*, http://cn.wikiquote.org/wiki/Anne_Frank. Last accessed March 11, 2010.

57. "Test Your Happiness: Psychologists Say It Is Possible to Measure Your Happiness," BBC News, http://news.bbc.co.uk/2/hi/programmes/ happiness_formula/4785402.stm. Last accessed March 11, 2010.

58. Jane Ogden, *The Psychology of Eating*, 2nd ed. (Chichester, UK: Wiley-Blackwell, 2010), 196.

59. James Bauman, "The Gold Medal Mind," *Psychology Today*, May 1, 2000, http://www.psychologytoday.com/articles/200005/the-gold-medal -mind. Last accessed March 11, 2010.

60. Ibid.

61. K. Takahashi, J. Tamura, and M. Tokoro, "Patterns of Social Relationships and Psychological Well-Being Among the Elderly." *International Journal of Behavioral Development* 21 (1997): 417, http:// jbd.sagepub.com/cgi/content/abstract/21/3/417, cited in Niven, *The 100 Simple Secrets*, 54.

62. "Why Dishing Does You Good: U-M Study," University of Michigan News Service, June 2, 2009, http://www.ns.umich.edu/htdocs/releases/ story.php?id=7181. Last accessed March 11, 2010.

63. E. Diener and M. Seligman, "Very Happy People," *Psychological Science* 13, no. 1 (2002): 82, http://www3.interscience.wiley.com/cgi-bin/full text/118922544/PDFSTART. Last accessed March 11, 2010.

64. Niven, *The 100 Simple Secrets*.

65. Ibid.

66. Carlin Flora, "A Boon for Caregivers," *Psychology Today*, November 1, 2003, http://www.psychologytoday.com/articles/200401/boon-caregivers. Last accessed March 11, 2010.

67. Flora, "A Boon for Caregivers"; S. Brown, R. Nesse, A. Vinokur, and D. Smith, "Providing Social Support May Be More Beneficial than Receiving It: Results from a Prospective Study of Mortality," *Psychological Science* 14, no. 4 (2003): 320–27, http://www.psychologicalscience.org/pdf/14_4Brown.cfm. Last accessed March 11, 2010.

68. Claudia Willis, "The New Science of Happiness," *Time*, January 17, 2005, http://www.time.com/time/magazine/article/0,9171,1015832-4,00.html. Last accessed March 11, 2010.

69. Lyubomirsky, *The How of Happiness*, 127.

70. Elizabeth Svoboda, "Pay It Forward," *Psychology Today*, July 1, 2006, http://www.psychologytoday.com/articles/pto-20060719-000008.html. Last accessed March 11, 2010.

71. Ibid.

SECTION 5

1. "Mohandas Karamchand Gandhi," *Wikiquote*, http://en.wikiquote.org/ wiki/Mahatma_Gandhi.

2. U.S. Census Bureau, *Selected Social Characteristics in the United States*: 2006–2008, http://factfinder.census.gov/servlet/ADPTable?_bm=y &-geo_id=01000US&-qr_name=ACS_2008_3YR_G00_DP3YR2&-ds_name =ACS_2008_3YR_G00_&-_lang=en&-_sse=on. Last accessed March 12, 2010.

3. Henry Ricciuti, "Single Parenthood, Achievement, and Problem Behavior in White, Black, and Hispanic Children," *Journal of Educational Research* 97, no. 4 (March–April, 2004).

4. "On Mother's Day, a Hopeful Finding for Single Mothers and Their Children from a Cornell Researcher," *Cornell News*, May 6, 2004, http://www.news.cornell.edu/releases/May04/single.parents.ssl.html. Last accessed March 11, 2010.

5. Ibid.

6. Saleebey, *Strengths Perspective*.

7. Mohit Midha, "The Tigress as a Mother," in *Wildlife of India*, http://www.wildlywise.com/tiger_mother.htm, reprinted with permission.

8. Roger Ebert, "Children of Heaven," February 5, 1999, http://rogerebert.suntimes.com/apps/pbcs.dll/article?AID=/19990205/REVIEWS/902050301/1023. Last accessed March 11, 2010.

9. Barack Obama, *Dreams from My Father: A Story of Race and Inheritance* (New York: Random House, 2004), xvi.

10. "Positive Parenting Can Have Lasting Impact for Generations," Oregon State University, News and Communication Service, September 1, 2009, http://oregonstate.edu/ua/ncs/archives/2009/sep/positive-parenting -can-have-lasting-impact-generations. Last accessed March 15, 2010.

11. "Quotations about Mothers," QuoteGarden, http://www.quotegarden.com/mothers.html. Last accessed March 11, 2010.

12. Wikipedia, "Pygmalion Effect," http://en.wikipedia.org/wiki/Pygmalion _effect. Last accessed March 11, 2010.

13. Mike Celizic, "Mom Lets Nine Year Old Take Subway Home Alone," TodayShow.com, April 3, 2008, http://www.msnbc.msn.com/id/23935873/v; Last accessed March 11, 2010. Amy Douthett, "Hey, Parents, Leave Those Kids Alone!" STATS.org, July 17, 2009, http://www.stats.org/stories/2009/hey_parents_july17_09.html. Last accessed March 11, 2010.

14. Lisa Belkin, "Let the Kid Be," *New York Times Magazine*, May 29, 2009, http://www.nytimes.com/2009/05/31/magazine/31wwln-lede-t.html. Last accessed March 11, 2010.

15. Douthett, "Hey, Parents."

16. Hara Estroff Marano, "A Nation of Wimps," *Psychology Today*, November 1, 2004, http://www.psychologytoday.com/articles/200411/nation-wimps/. Last accessed March 11, 2010.

17. Ibid.

18. Marano, *A Nation of Wimps: The High Cost of Invasive Parenting* (New York: Broadway Books, 2008), 3.

19. Marano, "A Nation of Wimps."

20. Ibid.

21. Reid, "The Nocebo Effect."

22. Y. Ikemi and S. Nakagawa, "A Psychosomatic Study of Contagious Dermatitis," *Kyushu Journal of Medical Science* 13 (1962): 335–50.

23. Kirsch, "Challenging Received Wisdom."

24. Dr. Thomas Gordon, *Parent Effectiveness Training: The Proven Program for Raising Responsible Children* (New York: Three Rivers Press 2000), p. 43. All excerpts from this source are reprinted with permission from the Linda Adams Trust.

25. Ibid.

26. Belkin, "Let the Kid Be."

27. Carl Honore, "Under Pressure," http://www.carlhonore.com/?page_id=5. Last accessed March 11, 2010.

28. Gordon, *Parent Effectiveness Training*, 38.

29. Ibid., 39.

30. Georgia Orcutt, "Unspoil Your Child: Raise a Child, Not a Tyrant," Parenthood.com, http://www.parenthood.com/article-topics/unspoil _your_child_raise_a_child_not_a_tyrant.html. Last accessed March 11, 2010.

31. Gordon, *Parent Effectiveness Training*.

32. Ibid., 115.

33. Ibid., 135.

34. Ibid., 143.

35. Marano, *A Nation of Wimps*.

36. Ibid., 14.

37. Ibid., 117.

38. "Happiness is a collective—not just individual—phenomenon," Harvard Medical School, December 4, 2008. http://web.med.harvard.edu/sites/RELEASES/html/christakis_happiness.html. Last accessed March 11, 2010.

39. "Study: Happiness Is Contagious," CBSNews.com, December 4, 2008, http://www.cbsnews.com/stories/2008/12/04/health/main46493 93.shtml. Last accessed March 11, 2010.

40. Nancy Shute, "Good Parents, Bad Results," *U.S. News and World Report*, June 12, 2008, http://health.usnews.com/articles/health/living-well -usn/2008/06/12/good-parents-bad-results.html?PageNr=3. Last accessed March 11, 2010.

41. "U of Minnesota Researcher Finds Materialism in Children and Adolescents Linked to Self-Esteem," University of Minnesota, November 26, 2007. http://www.eurekalert.org/pub_releases/2007-11/uom-uom112007.php. Last accessed March 11, 2010; Lan Nguyen Chaplin and Deborah Roedder John, "Growing up in a Material World: Age Differences in Materialism in Children and Adolescents," *Journal of Consumer Research*, December 2007, Vol. 34, No. 4: pp. 480–93. http://www.journals.uchicago.edu/doi/abs/10.1086/518546?journalCode=jcr. Last accessed March 11, 2010.

42. Nathaniel Branden, *The Art Of Living Consciously: The Power of Awareness to Transform Everyday Life* (New York: Simon & Schuster, 1997), 172.

43. Nathaniel Branden, "What Self-Esteem Is and Is Not," http://www .nathanielbranden.com/ess/exc04.html. Last accessed March 11, 2010.

44. Jim Taylor, "Parenting: Don't Praise Your Children," *Psychology Today*, September 3, 2009, http://www.psychologytoday.com/blog/the-power -prime/200909/parenting-dont-praise-your-children. Last accessed March 12, 2010.

45. "Average Home Has More TVs than People," USATODAY.com, http://www.usatoday.com/life/television/news/2006-09-21-homes-tv_x.htm. Last accessed March 15, 2010.

46. "How Teens Use Media: A Nielsen Report on the Myths and Real-ities of Teen Media Trends," *Nielsen*, June 2009, http://blog.nielsen.com/ nielsenwire/reports/nielsen_howteensusemedia_june09.pdf. Last accessed March 12, 2010.

47. Alice Park, "Study: TV May Inhibit Babies' Language Develop-ment," *Time*, June 1, 2009, http://www.time.com/time/health/article/ 0,8599,1902209,00.html?xid=rss-health. Last accessed March 12, 2010; D. A. Christakis, J. Gilkerson, J. A. Richards, F. J. Zimmerman, M. M. Garrison, D. Xu, S. Gray, and U. Yapanel, "Audible Television and Decreased Adult Words, Infant Vocalizations, and Conversational Turns: A Population-Based Study," *Arch Pediatr Adolesc Med*, June 2009, 163(6):554–58. http://archpedi .highwire.org/cgi/content/abstract/163/6/554. Last accessed March 12, 2010.

48. Ibid.

49. Joel Schwarz, "Baby DVDs, Videos May Hinder, Not Help, Infants' Language Development," *University of Washington News*, August 7, 2007, http://uwnews.washington.edu/ni/article.asp?articleID=35898. Last accessed March 12, 2010.

50. Alvin Rosenfeld, MD and Nicole Wise, *The Over-Scheduled Child: Avoiding the Hyper-Parenting Trap*, (New York: St. Martin's Griffin, 2001), 252.

51. Richard Louv, "The Benefits of Boredom," August 16, 1999, http:// www.connectforkids.org/node/121. Last accessed March 12, 2010.

52. James Steyer, *The Other Parent: The Inside Story of the Media's Effect on Our Children* (New York: Atria Books, 2002), 5.

53. "Exercise," johnratey.com. http://www.johnratey.com/newsite/ index.html. Last accessed March 12, 2010; Mary Carmichael, "Health: Can Exercise Make You Smarter?," *Newsweek*, March 26, 2007, http://www .newsweek.com/id/36056/page/2. Last accessed March 15, 2010.

54. Frances E. Kuo, PhD and Andrea Faber Taylor, PhD, "A Potential Natural Treatment for Attention-Deficit/Hyperactivity Disorder: Evidence From a National Study," *Am J Public Health*, September 2004: 94(9): 1580– 86. http://www.ncbi.nlm.nih.gov/pmc/articles/PMC1448497/. Last accessed March 12, 2010.

55. Wikipedia, "Nature Deficit Disorder," http://en.wikipedia.org/wiki/ Nature_deficit_disorder#cite_note-2. Last accessed March 12, 2010;

Richard Louv, "Last Child in the Woods," http://richardlouv.com/. Last accessed March 12, 2010.

56. "History of the Touch Research Institute," Touch Research Institute. http://www6.miami.edu/touch-research/About.html. Last accessed March 12, 2010.

57. "Children Who Have Frequent Family Dinners Less Likely to Use Marijuana, Tobacco, and Drink Alcohol," The National Center on Addiction and Substance Abuse at Columbia University, press release, September 15, 2008, http://www.casacolumbia.org/absolutenm/templates/PressReleases .aspx?articleid=535&zoneid=68. Last accessed March 12, 2010.

58. "Albert Einstein," *WikiQuote*, http://en.wikiquote.org/wiki/Albert _Einstein.

59. Leo Calvin Rosten, *The New Joys of Yiddish* (New York: Three Rivers Press, 2001), 233.

60. Wikipedia, "Leo Rosten," http://en.wikipedia.org/wiki/Leo_Rosten.

SECTION 6

1. "Why I Love Being a Single Mother," *Mothering*, http://www .mothering.com/discussions/showthread.php?t=219427. Last accessed March 12, 2010.

Index

About the Author

SANDY CHALKOUN is a lawyer and the owner of her own legal training business in Montreal. She travels across Canada teaching law seminars to business people.

She became a single mother when her son was 11 months old. She refused to accept the old stereotype of a single mother as uneducated, poor, miserable, traumatized, and unstable. Instead, she decided to see herself as a tiger in charge of her young.

She spent six years on her own, learning about the latest research on the science of happiness, positive psychology, and other disciplines. She learned how to transform her feelings of fear, anxiety, guilt, and low self-esteem into a positive, confident attitude and feelings of freedom. She developed 22 powerful Happiness Strategies for single mothers to improve the quality of their lives and those of their children. She now lives with her son, her ideal new partner, and a new baby daughter in Canada.